# $\mathcal{A}$SCENSION

## ANGEL MESSAGES

*by*

## MELANIE BECKLER

*For you.*
*May you fully remember*
*the brilliance of the light that you are.*

# Contents

## Author's Note ~

This book offers you the opportunity to receive direct channeled teaching from the angelic realms. To gain the most benefit from this book, think of it as a reading meditation. As you read these words, imagine that you are hearing them, as if the angels were speaking directly to you.

Each of the angel messages in this book carries a beautiful angelic frequency alongside the words. As you *listen to the guidance from the angels* while you read, pay attention to your subtle senses and feelings, as you will very much be in the presence of angels.

You may even want to imagine yourself in a peaceful location in nature while you read, or inside a beautiful sanctuary of light where you are in the direct presence of your guides and angels.

You *are* in the direct presence of your guides and angels who lovingly and powerfully assist you in tuning into the healing, frequency and wisdom available for you now.

*~Melanie Beckler*

## Invocation ~

*At this time I invite you to join me in finding a comfortable and relaxed position. Take a deep breath, and begin to shift your awareness so that you're focusing within.*

*I ask that we be surrounded with Divine white light and with each of our Spirit Guides and Angels of healing, love, light and protection. Please come in, protect us, uplift our energy, and assist us in tuning into the knowledge, wisdom and truth which will most serve now, for the highest and greatest good according to Divine Will, and so it is.*

*As you read these words, allow yourself to naturally rise up in consciousness into direct presence with Source, God, and with All That Is.*

*I now call upon the highest, best and most loving possible channeling guides who can most serve.*

*Please come in, connect and channel through me now...*

# Preface

## ~ *Archangel Michael*

G reetings dear one. I Archangel Michael am present with you now. I am pleased to connect with you now energetically and with frequency, through this channel who receives these words as a stream of consciousness alongside her own.

Melanie has agreed before birth and consciously in this now, to step back, to step into a state of love, a state of awareness and presence, to receive this guidance from beyond the veil. This guidance from the angelic and spiritual realms for the purpose of reawakening humanity to the brilliance which lies within at an individual and at the level of the collective.

The time for reuniting with inner Divine wisdom, knowledge, and light is now.

Through awakening and realigning more fully with love through your choices, your actions and your presence, Divine inner wisdom, knowledge, truth, and insight are able to be accessed incrementally when you are ready.

You have made it to a point in the ascension process that the sky is the limit, so to speak. There's no going back now, there's only going further in expanding consciously, in remembering and in opening the vault of ascension energy which is collectively and individually held within.

And so continue further on your ascension path, one step at a time, one moment at a time and reading one word at a time as you return to love.

Conscious awakening on the ascension path is choosing to walk the path of love. It is returning to love in the present moment.

Indeed love in the moment is the key to preparing yourself to access the information stored within you, the information of your higher consciousness and your soul which has the potential to create positive change on an individual and collective scale.

You have already progressed far and yet you have merely taken a step in the grand scope of how far you are able to travel, of how high you are able to lift, of how advanced you are able to evolve, ascend, and become illuminated as the spiritual being that you are.

You are ready to fully awaken as the spiritual being that you are, as Divine presence manifest within your physical form. This is possible for you in this lifetime still.

Ascension through your return to love, through your presence in the moment, through your full awakening is possible for you now.

One step at a time.

# Introduction

## ~*Spirit Guide Odrian*

*G*reetings to you, Dear One, I am Odrian and I greet you in this present moment, in this very time. I greet you with your team of guides and angels and with an entire entourage of beings of unconditional love and light. Here enter these ascended masters and teachers from the spiritual realms, these angels and archangels, these guides and indeed your beloved ancestors who are all entering into this present time and space to unite with you energetically. This is made possible through the Oneness which you are aware of that connects all.

Know that I, Odrian, am indeed a spirit guide of the Divine light. Indeed I have lived various manifestations within the physical realm, on Earth and within other physical manifestations. I am ascending as you are. I have ascended now in spirit into full Oneness with God, with Divine light, with Sananda, who you may know as Jesus, and with All That Is.

I am so pleased to connect with you as are your many friends in the spiritual realms – many guides and angels who have gathered here and now to make this link with you. They are all present, and so together we broadcast our love, and together we assist you in linking directly with God, directly with the Divine.

There are some who would say there is no purpose in connecting with Angels. "Go up directly and seek God," they say. We say to you, "Yes, go up directly and seek God, go up directly and seek Source, go within and connect directly with the Divine for you are One with this always."

But know also that just as you have a purpose here on Earth – to grow, to evolve, to learn, to share, to teach, to witness and to serve – so too do angels and spirit guides have a purpose. We continue to evolve and learn and grow. Many, including the Archangels and I, chose at a point on a past timeline to fully unite with the Divine will.

We have surrendered our free will that you experience from within your physical realm – the free will to choose something that is out of alignment with the will of God. But you as a human being have this right. We in the realms of spirit guides and angels who serve the light have surrendered this free will and are acting according to Divine inspiration at all times.

My being here now is not serving myself, it is serving the Divine will to share the teachings of the Divine with you now, to share my experience and the experience of the collective consciousness of beings who have lived as humans and ascended, and who are with you now.

You are at the brink of the next level of becoming. You are ascending indeed and we wish to impart wisdom and guidance and indeed frequency to serve you according to the Divine will. Not for our own motivations, but for the highest and greatest good according to Divine will.

The energy of Source, of the Divine, of God which is indeed all-knowing, all-seeing, all-encompassing and which has given you the opportunity of free will to make choices, to learn, to participate in this grand classroom and experience of life. You are at a threshold collectively indeed. You have crossed through the doorway. You have crossed a point which many thought you would not cross. You have passed the point in time which was mirrored at the time of Atlantis when the civilization was destroyed. Many thought your civilization now would repeat that experience which you did not, and not because there aren't those among you who wish for that to happen. Collectively it was your choice as humanity and collectively you chose love.

The scale has been tipped in the direction of light and love, and so you have crossed through the doorway of light, you are on the other side and yet you remain at the threshold still and so we connect with you in this present moment.

We connect with you with words and with frequency to guide you forward, for while the journey before you is new to your eyes, it has been walked by many. Indeed, it is familiar to many of the Archangels who you know and love who have indeed lived physical lives and ascended to their current frequency and vibration.

The pathway has been paved indeed by many of the figures you know and love in history such as Jesus, such as Mother Mary, such as Buddha, who have walked the path of ascension to reunite fully with God, to be one with all.

And this pathway which has been illuminated with light is the journey you are embarking upon now, and you have crossed through the doors which open to the next level of illumination, of ascension, of the new paradigm.

Within this new paradigm, humanity, Earth and all are ascending. Humanity, Earth and all are changing, re-aligning with Divine will. Do not worry! You are not being asked to give up your free will. You are simply collectively recognizing the path of Divine will and you are embarking in this empowering, uplifting, rewarding, inspiring direction.

When you express the love that you are, when you recognize the love that you are, when you live in love, as love, mindful of love, then the blessings of love elevate the entire playing field. Love elevates the current paradigm, elevates the vibration you radiate and elevates the vibration which is mirrored back to you

And on this path the potential is present for the total healing and replenishment of your planet, for the total healing and replenishment of your physical vessel and indeed, your advancement forward collectively opens up new frontiers for you as a galactic citizen.

Instead of thinking you are a citizen of a particular country within a divided Earth, you will recognize that you are a citizen of Earth within a greater galactic community filled with beings at differing levels of evolution and consciousness, some of whom are in physical bodies quite similar to your own. Others exist in a state of being that is much more like I, Odrian – a complete presence in spirit. And as your consciousness expands now, you are able to see that all this is true and you are not only a citizen of Earth, separate from all these beings, but you are one with all.

One part of transitioning through this doorway, of entering the new paradigm is becoming aware of the greater extent of dimensions. It has been said that there are twelve dimensions you can access from within your physical realm, but in fact there are infinite, there are unlimited dimensions and planes of existence – parallel realities in infinite directions across the lines of time which you are connected to.

To get a bit more complex and abstract for a moment, there are past lives which you have lead in these alternate dimensions of experience on alternate planets which exist on a different timeline, and these experiences are continuing to unfold now. And so you on physical Earth as a soul within a physical form are not only here but you also exist multi-dimensionally throughout time and space in other expressions, in other forms, in spirit, in other places. Your soul lives parallel experiences. These are parallel adventures of learning through consciousness, parallel lessons and lives. And yet the vast plethora of what you are is all connected, it is all one.

To think about the power of your choice is to think that your choice here and now ripples outward and touches all of existence. Your choice in this life influences your soul's experience in that parallel expression and in a more physical sense, in terms of Earth, your choice influences all humanity and all beings on the planet. Your choosing love has a tremendous impact.

So if you have been feeling a bit funny, feeling a bit weird, know that you are simply re-calibrating to this new energy and climate. You are recalibrating to the fact that an infinite amount of alternate dimensions are now within your reach, and your balance within this transition, your key to unlock the new technologies and opportunities and frequencies available according to Divine will lies within you.

Your heart remains the portal to access the higher dimensions. Your heart remains the portal to access the angelic realms and more. Your heart remains the portal to link directly with God. And your heart remains the portal which activates your light body and allows you as a spiritual being, as a being experiencing parallel dimensions in spirit, at the soul level, to energetically travel, to astrally travel and to claim the knowledge, the experiences, the blessings of these parallel existences.

We realize this is a bit abstract, for your mind can truly only comprehend what is already known.

You are standing at this new frontier with infinite realms of unknown before you, and so you cannot expect to instantly understand and know it all. You can simply take your next step by opening more fully to experiencing the magic of God, the infinite light of the Divine, which manifests through you.

Did you really think the unlimited, all-powerful, omnipotent Divine source was only manifesting in one dimension, one place and time?

Across the lines of time, across time and space, across vast universes and dimensions and planes, Divine will is unfolding. We – your team of helpers and spirit guides – applaud you and encourage you for being here now, for being willing to walk the path of love in alignment with Divine will and to move into the new paradigm which holds so much beauty, so much potential for the new Earth, and which ripples out through all that is – through everything, through the one Source, God, infinitely manifest through I, through you, through us.

We are one and we shall meet again.

# 1

# Illuminating Your Ascension Path

## ~ *Archangel Metatron*

*D*ear one, I am Archangel Metatron. I greet you now with love and with Divine well-being.

Although changes in life often seem turbulent and unknown, it is through the progression of changes that your highest good, the blessings and, indeed, the miracles can unfold.

You are at the precipice of another stream of changes flowing into your being. Change stirs within the earth. It stirs within the greater field of consciousness and within your own life path, but do not be afraid. Instead, know and remember that you are a Divine spiritual being in physical form. You are here in life on planet earth not to effortlessly glide on autopilot through the present moment, but to be an active participant in manifesting your highest and greatest good, in learning your lessons, in accomplishing your purpose.

Life unfolds one moment at a time. Love moves you in the direction of increased frequency and well-being. Fear drains your energy, lowers your vibration, and brings you to manifest more to be fearful of. This is your authentic choice: love or fear. It has been and is present and available to you at every moment, in every scenario — every second, every action offers the opportunity for a reaction and you have the choice of love or fear.

Ascension is a process which you, the earth and all beings and inhabitants of the planet earth are undergoing. It is the process of moving in the direction of love, a process of raising in vibration not once and for all, but moment by moment. It is a progression which us unfolding, ever in the present moment. You are able to reach new heights of Divine light and frequency and personal power, from within.

You are a spiritual being, first and foremost. You have been born into this physical realm to experience the blessings of the ascension path — not the effortless path, not the autopilot path, but the ascension path, which encompasses aspects of a spiritual path, of being spiritual, of being connected to spirit. But it expands further. The ascension path involves facing all fear and darkness and density within you, and dealing with blockages and doubts and density, healing the past, present and future aspects of yourself in order to retain the full light of the Divine.

The archangels, ascended masters and your spirit guides who are present here with you now are vibrating with the presence of the Divine. These ascended beings of increased love and vibration will assist you now and always in walking this path of returning to the full connection with God and with All That Is, to the full connection with the infinite "now" that is ever in the present moment.

And so your ascension path, which, yes, continues to accelerate, is primarily twofold. Cleansing that which is not, and integrating that which is: love, life, compassion, beauty and Divine in this present moment. Integrating that which is in alignment with your furthered ascension, raising in vibration, aligning with your authentic path and purpose, living vibrantly inspired and alive involves not only turning away from your ego and from your personal doubts and fears and frustrations but also dissolving densities, blockages and tensions into the light and replacing them with the high-vibration counterparts of love, compassion, knowledge, wisdom, truth and light.

As you shift, as you personally reach the tipping point where your light and love in the present moment outweigh your fear and insecurity and negativity, you act as a beacon, a signal, an alarm clock or a lighthouse for others who have in spirit chosen to ascend but in the physical realm have not yet begun the process of releasing the lower-vibration frequencies from their life. These lower-vibration frequencies include habits and addictions. They also include thoughts, feelings and emotions, beliefs and intentions, as well as energies.

The grip of belief, of thought and of fear is strong and tenacious upon many. It holds them fast asleep and trapped within the cage of negativity — the limits and confines of material reality. But as you know, as you have glimpsed and experienced, the realms of spirit are now open for you and the path through the veil of illusion has been paved, the gate is left open. You are ready to return home in the present moment and to experience, radiate and honor the Divine light within you that is within everything.

It is easy to become caught up in what is wrong in your world. Yes, there is much that needs changing. Yes, there is much suffering and cruelty and negativity present here still. Know that your inner state of being is mirrored by the world outside and around you. And so your ascension work is fundamental in shifting that which is in physical reality, which is on the lower-vibrational scale. And your work in consciousness prepares you for your high-vibration work as an ascended physical being, for meditating and self-release and prayer and preparation are essential but are not all-inclusive for those spiritual beings who walk the ascension path in physical form.

Action in a physical sense is required, indeed. But through your meditation and preparation you are able to know your course of action and you are able to remain in love while engaging and changing the harsh or negative aspects present within physical reality. Remember that your choice makes all the difference — your choice in every moment, the grand choice, the ultimate choice. Love or fear may not always seem this clear-cut and this is why we encourage you to calm your mind, to take control of your status, to meditate and be present and clear out all fear and density and negativity still residing within you so that the path of love and compassion, of serving others and the earth naturally aligns with your being so that your choice — even when you are not fully aware — is in alignment with your ascension path. Your ascension path leads you in the direction of full awareness and full knowledge of your choice in every moment.

Love even your challenges, for you often grow far more from a challenge than from a state where everything is going well. Love the challenges and receive the insight and blessings contained therein. Don't think, *"Why me? Why must I experience this challenge?"* Instead, ask *"Why this? Why this challenge now? What*

*is my lesson in this challenge? What is the blessing in this challenge?"*
This perspective will help you to claim the seeds of power, the granules of light, the codes of consciousness and of frequency available for you amidst the challenge in the present moment.

This cleansing of old energy, making way for the brilliance of the inner light that is you is important work not to be completed once and then be over with. It is to be returned to and repeated. And so at this time as you imagine an orb of Divine white light above you and imagine that this orb begins to pour down a waterfall of white light around you. Light cleansing your mind, body, spirit, and expanding outward to cleanse your home and your space, your neighborhood, city and state, to cleanse your personal being and all whom you are in contact with, cleansing everything.

Let your awareness be directed to an area which you have been holding onto which does not serve, a habit or belief, or pattern of thought. This can be whatever is standing in the way of you reaching the next level of your ascension light, of your authentic power, of opening and blossoming as the Divine lotus of light frequency that you are. Notice it and be aware, for with awareness, release is simple. Release happens in a moment. Density is banished and fear dissolved, judgment eliminated and presence, Divine light and beauty brightly shine from within.

Notice the orb of light above you releasing another surge of light, a waterfall of light. It soothes you, rejuvenates your being and replenishes any energy which has been strained or tensed amidst recent challenges. Remember that your challenges contain blessings and opportunities for growth. They present opportunities to take leaps forward on your ascension path of aligning with the full light that you are through love which is all around you now cleansing and uplifting, inspiring and purifying.

And now with a burst of light your inner, authentic being brightly shines through, filling up your energetic being with light, your aura with light. This light from within fuels your body, mind, and spirit, which aligns blessings on your path. This empowers you to continue on your path of becoming better, lighter, more authentic, more loving, more in alignment with the Divine every day, in every way, for the highest and greatest good. You are cleansed and uplifted, you are empowered and inspired to carry on, to go further, to continue forward in walking your authentic path of ascension, reuniting, being the Divine spiritual being that you are in physical form.

I am Metatron. See the Divine light in you. Let it build and grow and shine. Nurture your Divine light with your choice, with your belief, with your thought, with your return to love in this moment and every moment.

# 2

# Ascension Activation
# of Divine Love

## ~ *Archangel Michael*

Greetings, beloved one. Indeed, I am Archangel Michael and I greet you now with Divine love, with uplifted energy, with Divine frequency from the higher realms which you are moving into, ascending into, lifting into consciously and actively now.

Take a moment to breathe freely and relax and become aware of your surroundings. Pay attention to any sounds, patterns of energy or distractions which are going on around you. Acknowledge what is there and now turn away from the distractions. For this moment turn inward and away from the outside world and the smells, sights and sounds. As you read, focus within, open up your heart and enter in. Let go, breathe and relax.

Let your mind become still and calm, letting your heart and your energy become activated and opened through your heart, through your subtle senses. You, beloved one, are now able to directly access Divine light, ascension energy, healing and vibration of the spiritual realms direct from the Divine source and from your higher self. That part of you that is one with

God, one with Divine energy, one with everything. It is tapped into infinite knowledge and intelligence from the higher realms. Not in terms of language, which is somewhat limiting in this regard — a construction of the physical realm and the third dimension.

Lift now above the realm of language, of words and thoughts into the experience of energy. Sense the vibration and patterns of frequency which are all around you and which you are lifting into. We describe this through language as love, as healing, as well-being, as high vibration, as ascension. But using language limits the experience. And so for this moment allow your mind to be calm and your heart to be activated and open. Allow your spiritual being to sense, know and understand through your own interpretation system this energy of the Divine and of the higher realms that you are connected with, indeed, connected with always.

And as you consciously, actively tune in, you invite it into your being. Breathe freely and allow the energy of the Divine, manifested through earth, air, fire, water and ether to flow throughout your being. Allow this Divine energy to flow along your spinal column and open and activate your energy, to release blockages. Allow this Divine energy to flow all the way from the earth's core below you upward to the infinite supply of Divine light above you. You are a conduit, a channel between that allows the energy to flow. And as this energy flows unblocked, untampered with and unhindered you unfold and blossom into the metaphorical lotus flower of awakening that you are, blossoming in this moment into your full potential.

Your Christed self, your higher spiritual being that is present, aware, conscious and one with Source — with God — with the Divine, with Earth, with all beings, with everything. Experience outside of your normal senses and outside the realm of language and thought. Experience beyond color, texture, sound and taste. Witness beyond seeing, hearing and knowing. Breathe freely, be present and energized, and be one with the light of the higher realms. Unite with the energy of your authentic ascended being.

Your higher self outside of space and time has progressed further on the path of ascension before you, and has achieved the best and the ultimate of what you wish to be possible as an ascended master, those inner inklings and nudges and dreams of what it means to ascend, and everything that this means to you. There is a part of you that has achieved this and more, and you are communing with that now, you are linking with it and you are honoring it now by embracing it. And for this moment allowing the possibility that not only is this possible, in an alternate timeline, in a future state of being, it already exists.

Now tune into this incredible light. Breathe freely and experience, shine... Pull the light of your higher self into your physical body, pull the energy of the Divine that is manifested in all the elements into your mind, body and spirit. Pull your spiritual power into this present moment — the power which activates the unique gifts and abilities bestowed upon you in this lifetime. The gifts which serve others and bring you joy, which contribute to the field of energy which creates all that is, manifesting and co-creating positive change. It is an uplifting and collective movement in the direction of love.

Experience the Divine energy of love, of awakened living, of authentic existence, co-connection and creation grounded in the present time in your being, in you and on earth in this present moment, moving forward into your life. Let yourself now tune into a mental image or picture of ways in which you would like to see your reality improve in terms of your heart's desire. Knowing that in every moment you are improving, advancing and moving forward as you respond with love.

With love in this moment you are unlimited. All is possible. Positively transforming your life and zooming way out, releasing the earth from negative influences, from corruption and coercion, aligning humanity, earth and everything with Divine love.

You are supported, blessed, protected and assisted as you walk this path. A love being, a love worker, Divine love manifesting tangibly, physically, spiritually, mentally and authentically in you in this moment and always. For another moment now, tune into the radiant bliss that you are connected with here and now, the Divine love, the spiritual power, the authentic being of your higher self and spirit. See the beauty of directly connecting with the Divine realms for yourself, and once more pull all this energy in, feel it flowing through your being, spinning internally, flowing through your mind, body, spirit, through your very cells, through the very matter of your being. Feel it infusing you with higher consciousness as it uplifts your vibration and assists you in progressing now on your path of ascension into living in a higher state of being in line with love, with joy, with that which you authentically represent, connected always to the source, God, to the Divine and to All That Is.

Feel, see, imagine, sense, know, smell, experience the wonder of this love and light. Pull it into your being and feel it grounded into this present moment, into your being, into your body, into the earth, anchoring through your connection to the earth and to All That Is. It activates your spiritual power, your clear sense of purpose and knowledge, your Divine resource of love and willingness and ability and ambition and motivation to choose love, to respond with love, to experience love beyond the confines of a word, beyond the confines of language, beyond the confines of the third dimension.

Imagine experiencing love in its highest possible vibration. This highest vibration is available to you now. Witness, choose, radiate, share and experience this. Anchor it into your life, into the physical realm, and create this outward ripple of the highest possible vibration, of Divine love radiating outward throughout everything. I, Archangel Michael, leave you with the blessing of Divine love, peace and serenity.

# Embody Your Divine Spirit

## ~ *Archangel Michael*

*B*eloved one, indeed, we are here. Your angels and as-cended masters and guides, and I, Archangel Michael, now speak unto you. At this time you are surrounded with Di-vine love, healing and frequency. Take this moment to tune in and experience your oneness with the light of the Divine, your oneness with All That Is.

Breathe and notice your feeling, your state of being, your point of resonance with this Divine frequency and energy that is now present. Open your heart, quiet your mind, see, hear, sense, know, feel, smell and experience the Divine light  all around you that you are a part of, that you are stepping into, radiat-ing, embodying and expressing from within your physical form. Bathe now in the light of the Divine.

This light shines above, behind, below, beside and in front of you. It soothes, nurtures and lifts up your being. Notice this connection with the Divine light. These frequencies and ener-gies are always here. You always have the ability to tune into and embody the light of your higher spirit, who is always one with the Divine.

And when you embody this light, you empower your creation with the attributes of the Divine — with love, compassion, patience, forgiveness, with light, with well-being, with bliss, with peace, with serenity. Feel yourself resonate with these qualities, feel your resonance with love, with tranquility, with compassion, and feel your resonance with fear, with separation. Which of these are you drawn to embody? Which of these feelings are connected to your higher spirit? Which are you drawn to exude and embody and embrace? Are you choosing this? In your life, are you choosing love and expansion and forgiveness and joy? For this is your choice.

This is always the choice for, you see, you are always creating. Whether you are creating from the perspective of the ego mind, weaving in energies of fear and separation and contraction, or whether you are creating from your Christed self, embodying the Divine spirit and creating love and harmony and well-being.

Whatever you are creating, consciously or unconsciously, from a connection with source or a connection with ego, from a connection with love or a connection with fear, your energy creates a ripple throughout consciousness, throughout humanity, throughout the earth. Your energy combines with the energy of others and together weaves the fabric of creation. This creates your experience. And so while we beings of light and love are available to help keep you on course, to help guide and assist you, to serve and to love, you are ultimately responsible for your own experience.

And so in our time together now, as we embody the qualities of the Divine, we encourage you to commit, to choose now and move forward to embody the qualities of the Divine for yourself, and this begins with awareness of what you are feeling and experiencing. Are you feeling and experiencing the density of the third dimension? Are you feeling and experiencing its chaos and hardship and struggle?

Step back. Why? You choose to engage in the frequency in this way, in the frequency of ego. Why give your ego the control? Step back. Step in to the awareness of your connection with God, with the Divine. Feel and experience this perspective now. Know that when you create from this point of clarity, from this point of connection with the Divine, your creation is embedded with the attributes and qualities manifested in this Divine spirit. Words carry vibration. Words are simply a description of energy.

And so are you creating and feeling love, peace and joy? Or rather fear, hardship and separation? Be aware of the difference in vibration of these two sets of words. Which do you choose to weave into your experience? Love or fear? And your choice creates your surroundings. The choice in the moment plants a seed of energy, creating a ripple outward so that when you serve and love, this energy flows outward and is mirrored back. And when you fear and doubt, the same occurs.

You have a huge opportunity now to link with the Divine, to infuse your consciousness with love, to embody your Divine spirit in every moment. Your path of ascension does not eliminate every challenge or lesson from your life, but when you look at it from the perspective that spirit does not and cannot know separation, you are able to understand that through your oneness and embodiment of spirit, manifesting those attributes of the Divine and living as the Divine being that you are, you eliminate the struggle. For there is no separation between you and the Divine. There is complete oneness between you and All That Is.

And through your choice of love, you infuse consciousness with the vibration of this choice. You infuse your life with this conscious experience. And then as individuals band together and consciously choose together to love, to meditate, to radiate peace and bliss and evolution, peace unfolds in your realm. Strive for clarity of mind to release the muddy, heavy thoughts and worries which manifest as tension, as stress, as disease in your realm.

Release these. Let go of them and choose the higher vibrational experience of stillness and awareness, and then allow a clear, focused, conscious and deliberate thinking to occur that contains the vibrational essence and attributes of the Divine, the energies which serve and uplift, which love and inspire, which ripple out from beyond you in a positive way that serves you and serves all. What do you choose? To live in love or fear? To embody the attributes of the Divine? Or to experience the qualities of ego mind? You are creating either way — you are contributing to creation either way. But tune into the knowledge of your choice before you were born, the contract you made with yourself, with your higher spirit, for your life here and now, that agreement to embody your spirit, to anchor the light, to live as the Divine spiritual being that you authentically are.

You have the opportunity if you would like to recommit to this contract, to this commitment between you and the Divine. Do you choose to embody the Divine in this life? Do you choose to live as an ascended being and integrate the new lights and frequencies? Do you choose to consciously create your world with your power of love? Your opportunity to choose is in every moment. Return to bliss, to love, to peace. We do not judge you when you choose the other way, but we see the fork in the road you have reached, the paths which lead both ways, and we humbly and lovingly invite you to choose love, to choose to embody your spirit, and to join us beings of light who embody the Divine qualities and attributes of understanding, wisdom, knowledge, certainty, creativity, abundance, clarity, love, gentleness, compassion, peace, joy, confidence, enthusiasm, wellbeing and love.

Now is your time to step into the light that you emanate, to choose awareness, presence and love. Take another moment to simply breathe, be, and imagine pulling the light of the Divine towards you, magnetizing your full Divine light to you, integrating your higher self's qualities and the unique ways in which you embody the Divine light. The unique gifts, spiritual abilities and power of the Divine manifest through you, through service, through action, through awareness and presence. Unite with the light of the Divine being that you are, align your mind, body and spirit now.

Now feel your energy grounding, flowing downward, anchoring to the earth, to the light at the earth's core, anchoring to All That Is and all that you are a part of, everything that you are creating within. In every moment assistance is available, but you have all that you need now to go within and quiet the voice of ego mind and to be present, aware, to integrate your spirit, your Divine spirit.

You are one with All That Is. Embody this magnificent, eternal, radiant light uniquely manifest through you within the physical world in this exciting time of mass accelerated change. As you ascend during your life, you allow your full light to shine, you live as a Divine being, overcoming challenges, choosing love after you catch yourself in fear, returning to the present moment of awareness one moment at a time. Know that each time it gets a little easier, each time you stay in the light a little longer and continue further knowing that you are loved, knowing that you are integrating, becoming one, aligning with spirit, and with the Divine.

I, Archangel Michael, and your team of guides and angels and ascended beings bow to the Divine in you, we honor the light that shines from you. We leave you with our love and blessing. And so it is.

# 4

# Link With
# The Divine Mind

## ~ *Archangel Muriel*

*G*reetings, indeed, I, Muriel, connect with you at this time with Divine frequency and healing to soothe emotions and expand your mind, to link you fully with the Divine. Understand that now and ever, indeed, you are connected with all of eternity. We shine light upon this link between your heart and mind and the Divine that is one. Relax and breathe freely and use your senses, let this union be felt. Let your conscious awareness begin to expand to perceive your current self and life with an expanded perspective and vision of the Divine mind.

Become aware that you are now in the perfect place to learn your life's lessons. Allow yourself to contemplate and understand all that you have learned already up to this point and as you allow yourself to release your attachment to past experiences, challenges, lessons and even blessings, you are allowed to claim the benefit of what has been before to carry forward with renewed wisdom, compassion, confidence and certainty to accomplish your purpose for this life, which is Divine. Indeed, you are guided at all times and have the conscious choice to tune in to this guidance or to retain your perspective in a more physical sense.

As you seek out the guidance of your spirit guides and angels in your life, this will flow through with increased clarity and frequency. And as you continue to act upon intuitive nudges and promptings, the blessings and miracles of spirit will align you with gifts and ideal circumstances for your service which can then come into being.

How you perceive your intuitive guidance is not to be read about or taught to you. This is something you have always contained but have blocked out to an extent. With your intention now you can declare to your team of guides, angels and spiritual beings, *"I am open to receive guidance from the Divine. I am open to my intuition manifesting to the next level. I clearly experience my intuition and will act upon guidance I receive."*

Take a moment now to simply let yourself focus on your breathing to consciously release the resistance from your mind and consciously release thoughts, emotions and past challenges into the light. Imagine that you are breathing in white light and imagine that you are exhaling and letting go of everything that blocks you from expanding your mind, from linking fully with the Divine mind, with increased awareness, clarity, confidence and certainty to manifest the highest, greatest extent of your life purpose, which is, of course, ever unfolding one step at a time. At every moment your mind is consciously and unconsciously creating.

You have the opportunity to consciously program your mind with the attributes, characteristics and thought patterns that you desire — those that will carry you forward into living with more love and joy, living more vibrantly, living more passionately, living more in alignment with the authentic truth of who you are, which includes perceiving beyond the veil and experiencing the truth of the Divine, experiencing and living your authentic truth and bringing blessings of well-being, of clarity, of love, of joy to the collective consciousness of humanity, bringing peace from inside of you, from your internal state of being and manifesting this outwards so that it ripples throughout your consciousness, bringing humanity closer to the tipping point of launching collectively into living in peace.

The power of your mind can influence and touch upon all areas of your life. You have the choice to coast on autopilot asleep and unaware or to contemplate what has been, releasing attachment to all that has been including what you have loved and enjoyed and choosing to blaze a new frontier, a new path forward towards positivity and enlightenment in your life now. This frequency of joy, love and enlightenment cannot help but touch the lives of those around you in an immediate sense and on the greatest scale imaginable.

It is a natural reaction for you to focus your mind on the challenges, destructive tendencies, collective fears and uncertainties concerning where humanity or where you as an individual are headed. This is natural, but not encouraged, for your focus, indeed, draws it into experience. And so we encourage contemplation and awareness, being aware of what you perceive as both good and bad, being aware of what lies on both sides of the light spectrum within you and around you. This awareness then allows you to find solutions to problems and align yourself with actions and intentions which you as an individual can consciously use to move forward into living and expressing the Divine mind and the attributes that lie therein here in the physical realm.

Let yourself once again focus on your breathing as the team of guides and angels around you that is unique to you — your team — stream a sphere of energy around you to uplift you in vibration. Specifically focusing on your mind to elevate your consciousness, increase your clarity and link your present mind and heart with the Divine mind and heart. This is bringing the elevated attributes of consciousness of the Divine mind into the present space and time, into your awareness, expanding your perspective, expanding the extent to which you can serve and influence. Expanding your mind and consciousness now, opening the doors to allow creative and original thought, inspired ideas, Divinely inspired actions and the full experience of your intuition. You are meant to make a difference both in your vibrant living and well-being and through your witnessing and interacting with the world, with humanity and with the beings around you.

Every moment is indeed an opportunity to increase your personal awareness. Increase your personal joy and vitality and well-being and energy, to live passionately and vibrantly, stepping into your role as a conscious servant of love, united as one with all life.

Be aware of the intricate web connecting everything, aware of your individual actions and the greater role they play in influencing and inspiring others, accelerating the awakening of the planet, accelerating the awakening within yourself, aware that this includes all — your greater self, your Divine self, which includes All That Is.

It is the healing and advancement of this greater self, the acceptance of the present stage of duality and its intricately planned purpose and role that allows you, dear being of light, to rise above the challenges of this dualistic plane and to live inspired, to live enlightened, aware of the one light and love that is everything. But even challenges and tragedies have a role in the greater awakening and return to love on both a collective and a mass scale. Your wisdom that experience has brought, now has a tremendous impact on accelerating the journey of humanity, away from struggle and back into love.

Indeed, know that your personal conscious expansion is the direct route to the awakening of all, to the knowledge and experience of being interconnected, leading towards conscious choices, actions and unfolding new paradigms.

Know that your mind has been linked and attuned to the Divine mind in this moment. As you move forward, allowing original thought, creativity and clarity to enter in, by releasing judgment, mindless chatter, doubt, and focusing upon the past it comes easily through the practice of meditation and awareness. Allow your denser thinking and scattered thoughts to fade away with new clarity and inspired vision entering in. This will carry you forward one step at a time into living collectively as One, living inspired, bringing essential transformation and upliftment to this entire earth realm.

You are paving the path which others will follow. Take your next step, ignite your fullest light, give yourself permission to live your authentic truth. This truth is not contained in a box nor can it be written onto a single page. You are vibrant, multidimensional, unique, and an inspired being of Divine light whose truth manifests across multiple dimensions in a variety of forms, all of which come more into focus as you consciously choose to act upon inspiration, to tune in to the guidance available to you, to be aware of the magnificent possibility for growth, for vibrant awakening, and for making a difference that comes through being alive.

If you are bored, drained and tired, it is because you are following someone else's vision for your life. Practice linking with the Divine mind to allow your true inspiration and knowledge of why you are here to come into focus. For it is your true purpose that makes you feel alive and excited and vibrant and joyful and all this is needed to usher humanity forward, to turn the page on the past and to step into a vibrant new future.

I, Muriel, now leave, streaming a final surge of Divine love and frequency your way like a tidal wave washing away doubt and insecurity so that you may align yourself with the confidence and certainty and knowledge and clarity of connection, linking your mind with the Divine mind for the highest and greatest good, for your own benefit and for the well-being of all across all dimensions and experiences of time in this very moment and throughout All That Is. You are blessed, loved and encouraged. Embark and move forward, for your time is now. I am complete and so it is.

# 5

# High Vibrational Attunement

## ~ Archangel Metatron

*G*reetings, beloved one. Indeed, I am Archangel Metatron, present here and now. I am broadcasting light, broadcasting an infinite supply of Divine frequency from the higher realms into your present space and time, into this very moment, to assist you in letting go of your ego mind just for now, and in letting go of rational thought, worry, stress, letting go and entering in.

And so imagine before you a blank slate and focus within. Visualize the doors of your heart opening wide as you consciously drop in, entering into the inner sacred space found within your open heart where you are able to access the infinite guidance of your heart and soul. Build upon this as you rise in light to experience your angels' vibration, those spiritual beings of love. The ascended masters and saints who guide you from the other side, who guide and support and love you unconditionally from the realms of spirit and ever so subtly align the blessings and synchronicities to you as you continue forward on your path.

When you ask for help and guidance, when you think upon these beings, these spiritual masters, and invite their essence and presence and love into your life, the synchronicities, alignments, guidance and Divine placements upon your path can be increased tenfold. This allows the miraculous, the extraordinary and the beautiful to be experienced by you at every moment, for these energies are always present all around you. This is the power of gratitude in noticing and appreciating what is beautiful, it attracts more beauty, magnificence and miracles into your experience.

This is the benefit in lifting up your vibration, which we will assist you with shortly. Lifting up your vibration is made possible at any moment through your thought, through your action, through your point of perspective. When you change the way you perceive what is happening around you, what is happening around you changes, indeed. Viewing reality through the lens of love allows love to be mirrored unto you in a vast array of possibilities and potential. When love is focused on it builds and grows. Again, love is truly available for you in an infinite supply from the Divine, from the angelic realms, from the ascended masters, from saints and from spirit guides. All you have to do is breathe freely and quiet your thoughts, not worrying if your mind does chime in bombarding you with thought.

When it does, let yourself focus upon that thought for a moment. Acknowledge the thought. Think or say to the thought, *"I see you, you are mine, I acknowledge you."* Don't judge yourself for having a thought, simply acknowledge the thought. You're then able to let it go and return to silence, stillness and calm, focusing within, breathing and letting go.

Feel your energy and all aspects of yourself, all your frequency and personal power gathering in this very moment in your heart's center. And now feel your energy grounding, essentially flowing downward and connecting you to the earth and to All That Is.

With this grounded, centered, calm, relaxed and aware perspective you are now ready and able, and if you are willing now, lift up. Imagine you are beginning to float upward. Your guides and angels simultaneously broadcast a frequency, supporting you in your journey upward, supporting you in journeying into the Divine realms and lifting into the realms of spirit, lifting in happiness and in love on the wings of your angels.

Go up, lift up, float up into the Divine realms of consciousness, rising in frequency. Imagine this is happening, imagine it is so. Perceiving the spiritual realms now not with your physical senses or with your imagination. Subtly feel the light, know and experience it: the Divine light that is, indeed, all around you.

Lift upward in it, breathe in the white light of the Divine which soothes your being, which calms your nerves, which eases any tension or anxiety and which elevates your vibration, paving the pathway for you to reconnect time and time again with the Divine realms where you are present here and now and where you are able to call upon your guides, your guardian angels, the saints and ascended masters who can best assist you in claiming the blessings available for you in every moment. They are present, indeed, and when focused upon your connection with them builds and grows.

Simply think or say now, *"Guides, angels, ascended masters, what insight, healing or wisdom do you have for me now?"* Imagine you're opening your heart wider and that you are opening your energy up to receive this blessing of frequency, this guidance and love. Let it in, breathe it in, embrace it, know it, understand it through this communion with these spiritual beings who love you unconditionally, who desire for nothing more than to assist you in living your authentic truth. Your truth that is joyful, radiant, well, inspired and fulfilling.

We hold this vision for you and through this connection which you have made with the Divine, your purpose is magnified before you. When you move in the direction of joy, of excitement and of passion, you are on track. When you express gratitude for the tiny aspects, the little things in your reality, they are able to grow and build. Love within every moment is the master path before you which allows new blessings into your life. It knows no limit. Again, there is an infinite supply of love, of the vibration that is miraculous available through your communion, connection, oneness with the Divine, with the angels, with the ascended masters, with All That Is.

At this time we invite the saint or ascended master who can best serve you to now step forward. This may be a being you are familiar with, who you have learned about or maybe someone new. Be willing to accept the quality and the frequency that this beloved guide offers you now. Become aware of their message to you, and of the meaning which this connection holds for you right now. Breathe and receive, it may be healing, encouragement, attunement, introduction, forgiveness or simply love.

Receive the blessing from the saint or ascended master, this being who has walked upon the earth and has seen reality through the perspective you use to view it, and who has mastered their lessons of life. And so this saint or ascended master is coming forward now to help you to master your lessons, your sole objectives and your purpose for being here in the classroom of life.

Mastery over your emotions, mastery in terms of mental control, mastery in terms of your physical vitality, mastery in terms of your spiritual connection are all possible. Mastery of life does not only mean making a lot of money or even being a spiritual person. Mastery of life includes every aspect, harmoniously interwoven together in a way which is fulfilling and empowering for you and for others. It is seeing the blessings all around you, within you, and in others, seeing the light in others, seeing the Divine in others and in everything. Mastery is the enlightened perspective you are able to shift into when you let go of fear and doubt.

Know that this shift benefits you and the ripple of positivity created from this serves all, for you are connected with all of humanity, with all beings, with everything. Your growth and commitment to increasing your vibration, expanding your joy, living love and living in a state of fulfillment and alignment with your souls desires allows this to become possible for others as well.

A small pebble dropped in the pool of infinite possibility creates a ripple of magnificent effect throughout the vast field of oneness that is all that you are a part of and one with, and so it is.

At this time feel your expanded sense of self, your connection to everyone and to everything returning to your individual aura, energy, and physical body. The energy of everything that is cleansed and purified and contained within your cells, within your whole, within your mind, body and spirit.

The energy of All That Is, the vast network of connections and life and love and gratitude and well-being is aligned in your being, compressed into a compact, high vibratory light being, spiritual being, alive, vibrant in physical form, in you.

You are so loved, blessed and lifted. Carry this light throughout your life, for doing so makes a tremendous difference. Choose love. Draw love to you and witness the connections of love building upon one another and expanding throughout all of existence.

I am Archangel Metatron. On behalf of the many guides and angels, ascended masters and saints present with you now, we bow to the Divine in you, to the Divine light that you are, to the magnificence, brilliance and love that you are. Live this truth. Express this light as the authentic, empowered, radiant spiritual being that you are.

# 6

# Cleansing, Intentions and Manifestation

## ~ Archangel Michael

*B*eloved, I am Archangel Michael and I am pleased to greet you now. As you read these words, allow yourself to focus inward. Release any thought or mind chatter that appears. Simply focus within, focus upon your heart and allow your heart to open to receive the full conscious and energetic benefit of our time here together now.

And so let us begin with a cleansing of mind, preparing for the work we will do together. Let your mind be still and calm. Imagine that as you read, your mind is focusing on an inner screen of white light — and that white light is all around you. Become aware of the screen of white light within your mind.

If you notice shapes or colors or symbols or images, this is fine. The point is to relax and to simply clear your mind of thought. With your inner mind, gaze upon the white light before you. Focus on these words which you are reading and relax into this present moment.

Breathe and let go as a special team of clearing and cleansing guides and angels come in to cleanse the realm of your mind, to clear out old thought patterns, systems of belief, and negative thought forms which all contain an energy and over time amass and clump together to weigh down your mind. An orb of white light is placed in the center of your mind and as it bursts open; your mind receives a cleansing of Divine light.

Breathe freely and allow this to occur by simply relaxing and remaining present, gazing upon the white light which is before your inner mind which is clearing, settling, calming your mind and making space in your mind for creative thought and new ideas.

Making a space where you can focus upon what you want, on your intentions and desires without being weighed down by past negativity, by thoughts of worry or fear or doubt or uncertainty. These are released now with the help of your cleansing team allowing clarity of mind to enter in.

At this time the orb of Divine light grows to encompass your entire body. Once again, the orb bursts open with light, filling your entire physical body with Divine white light and cleansing your physical form. This cleansing releases toxins at the cellular level which are pushed out and released into the light. The cleansing includes purging out thoughts, which are tied to your physical body and are manifesting in unpleasant ways, but are pushed out now in this burst of light and released into the light of the Divine. This cleansing of your physical body releases blockages, tensions and stress held within your being. At this time let yourself tense your entire body subtly, and then relax, and let go.

Feel the weight of tension being released from your being. Relax deeply and enter in as your physical body is cleansed. The orb of light now expands outward to encompass your energetic and spiritual being. The cleansing expands to include pulling upon any and all energetic cords which are draining you, present, past and future cords to others, to situations, to people, to places, to lives and to things.

These cords are pulled upon with the assistance of your cleansing team. And I, Archangel Michael, cut all cords with a sword of light, pulling out the roots, and the roots and cords and any and all residue are released into the white light of the Divine, fully and completely.

In a similar manner, all energetic blockages in your physical, mental or emotional being, in your spiritual body, in your ethereal or astral body are now highlighted. They are focused on and released into the light.

Let go of blockages and allow yourself to be illuminated from within. Open your heart wide as you focus within and release the tension and density and negativity, allowing the inner authentic light of your soul and spirit to shine through and illuminate you from within so the light outside of you cleanses and uplifts and the light inside you radiates and shines.

You are cleansing yourself from the inside out and the outside in. You are cleansing your mind, body and spirit with the assistance of your guides and angels and of the Divine. You are cleansing yourself of negativity and density in all forms, of any energetic attachments or earthbound attachments or energetic entities occupying your same space. These are now released into the light.

Look up, rise up and release into the light of the Divine with the assistance of the team of guides and angels here now. Any negativity remaining in any form — negative energetic imprints, hooks or blocks, any shards or clumps of negative energy which are attached to your being — are released into the light of the Divine now with the assistance of your guides and angels. You are supported by the Divine white light orb surrounding you you and by your inner flame of Divine light brightly shining inside. Take in another deep breath of white light, imagining that this light is fanning the flame of your heart.

And now when you exhale, imagine that light is pumped throughout your entire body, mind and spirit. The light fills your energy body, your mental, emotional and spiritual body so that you are filled within and without with white light, cleansed, purified and uplifted in vibration. Now draw your awareness to an orb of light below your feet, imagining that this light is flowing up, now cleansing and purifying each of your *chakras* as it flows up all the way from your root to your crown and up into the light.

As this happens, if you feel that there are any blockages of your *chakras*, imagine these blockages being released into the light. If there are any layers of dense energy, imagine them be-ing peeled away and released into the light, allowing the light of the core of the earth, the light orb below you, to flow up through all of your *chakras* all the way to your crown. Any blocks that energetically prohibit this flow are now released into the light of the Divine, allowing the light to flow upward out your crown at the top of the head. Up above the realms of the angels, above the realms of ancestors, above the spiritual realms into direct connection with Source, with All That Is, with God, with the Divine, who blesses you with cleansing now, with newly cleansed, clear, brilliant, luminescent energy of the

Divine, of unconditional love and radiant well-being.

Let this Divine energy flow down, in through your crown *chakra*, down through your third eye, your throat, your heart, your solar plexus, sacral, root, legs, feet, down as you ground to the core of the earth and this light from above flows down. It is like a cosmic Draino flushing your system of anything that does not serve, of anything that is not in alignment with your highest and greatest good, of anything which is not in alignment with Divine love. Release and ground, releasing yourself into the light of the core of the earth.

Breathe freely and know that you are surrounded with angels. You are supported by the Divine, you are loved, blessed and uplifted as you receive this powerful cleansing of mind, body and spirit. Experience the light at the core of the earth that you are one with, that you are a part of, that you are connected to at all times and in all places.

Be aware of this connection now with the light at the core of the earth and now, once again, let it flow up. This time unblocking a column of white light along your spine, a column of Divine white light extending up from below and out your crown at the top of your head. Go up with it and go off into the light, into the direct presence with Source and All That Is. You are a cleansed, radiant, spiritual being. In this moment imagine that you are gazing down upon your home, upon your physical location, as a surge of light frequency flows there now.

Remain in this perspective of a detached observer simply witnessing as the light of the Divine and your team of healing and cleansing guides and angels go in and cleanse your home, your office, your car, your building, your physical location.

Receive a cleansing of the Divine, releasing attachments and blockages and energies of negativity and density, as a burst of light in the center pushes out all that is not love, all that does not serve your highest and greatest good — all that is not in alignment with unconditional love, compassion and well-being. Love cleanses your physical location, releasing all blockages and stagnant energy into the light.

As you read these words all residues of arguments or tensions or experiences past are now cleansed and released into the light of the Divine fully and completely, allowing light to shine within the walls of your home and residence, allowing the vibration to be cleansed and uplifted, allowing the vibration to be modified so that it supports you as you walk your spiritual journey of ascension.

Your team of healing guides and angels who can most serve in achieving this cleansing fully and completely sweep the area, vacuuming along the walls, reaching into every cranny and corner and nook and crevice, every basement corner and attic rafter, every inch and square foot, cleansing this space with love and with Divine white light fully and completely for the highest and greatest good. And so it is.

And now, beloved one, from your current vantage point as observer connected to the Divine and to All That Is brightly shining with Divine light, we invite you to be guided to a belief which is currently hindering your further growth and the manifestation of your desires.

Allow a limiting belief to come into your awareness now.

This belief is simply something you accept with certainty, that you know to be true. What is it that you know to be true that perhaps is not serving you? What do you believe with conviction that is manifesting in an uncomfortable or unproductive way? What belief or knowledge do you have about yourself and your life experience that you would be better off without?

Tune in to this belief now, focus upon it, and witness as your team of healing guides and angels assist you in releasing it into the light. Think, *"I release you,"* and witness this limiting belief leaving your being. Let go and let God. Release the limiting belief, the knowledge or certitude which does not serve you. Let it go into the light and let it now be replaced with a belief that will serve you well, with the knowledge and certainty that you are loved and supported, that all is possible, that all is well, that you are a Divine being able to accomplish your dreams, goals and desires.

Let the void in which your limiting belief was held be replaced with a new and empowered belief. Witness this replacement now — an empowering belief downloading, anchoring into your being. And let us repeat this process once more.

From your perspective as an observer connected to the Divine and connected to All That Is within the realm of your open heart, tune in now with the assistance of your guides and angels and the direct presence of the Divine. Tune into a knowledge, a belief, an understanding about yourself or your life which you believe to be true but which does not serve you in what you desire to create or in the truth of who you are as a spiritual being.

Tune into a limiting belief that is acting as a block to your ability to manifest and your ability to rapidly progress in the direction of your goals. Tune into this limiting belief now. What is the limiting belief you are tuning into? Notice whatever comes into your mind — an image, an impression, a coherent sentence outlining the belief. Focus on this belief, feel and experience the essence of it, and now release the limiting belief into the light. Your guides and angels are at hand. They wrap it in wings of love and release this limitation, this perspective of what you can and cannot do into the light of the Divine.

Now, allow the void where the limiting belief was held to be filled with an empowering belief, a belief which serves your highest and greatest good. Allow this empowering belief to download into your being and notice that as it does your vibration automatically rises, for you are now filled with more light. A blockage in the form of a belief has been released.

Continue to accomplish this work, releasing the beliefs which do not serve you, for your beliefs combined with your thoughts, combined with your emotions and your actions create your experience. You are truly at a new point in space and time in which you have more power than ever before, more light energy than ever before available to you to manifest positive changes and to co-create your life experience.

This is why cleansing and releasing those past and outdated modes of thinking and believing and viewing your reality is so important. For infinite possibilities await you. Unlimited potential lies before you. You are only limited by your own beliefs and perspectives of inadequacy and the idea that you cannot do something. For the truth of the matter is, yes you can. You are one with the Divine and with All That Is, and due to this oneness, due to your miraculous light, you are able to create within this realm of one and bestow blessings in the outside world and in the lives of others and in your own experience.

Take a deep breath of air, of the white light which is all around, and exhale, letting go of any worry or attachment and of any uncertainty. Fully enter into this present moment and tune into your intuitive knowledge now. Tune into the intuitive knowledge of what you want. Tune into something you want to create in your experience in this next cycle of life. Tune into what you want to experience, to really love, to really live, to serve and exist, to thrive as the spiritual being in physical form that you are. From this vantage of being connected to your intuitive knowledge, what do you want to manifest and create?

Notice what comes up for you in response to this general question. Imagine that the essence of what you want is being compacted now into a small pearl, seed or crystal. The essence of this — your desire — compacted into a high-vibration bead which you now place energetically in a small bag and let go.

Refocus upon your heart now. Open up your heart and through your intuition and through your direct connection with the Divine, with your higher self, your soul guidance, what do you desire to experience in this next cycle of life? What experience does your heart call out for?

This could be an experience of being of service, a spiritual experience, a life experience, an activity you'd like to experience, or a place you'd like to visit. What experience do you desire?

Tune into the energy and essence of this. What does it look like, feel like, taste like? What does it vibrate like? Tune into the essence and the energy of your desired experience and imagine that the energy is being compacted. This future experience is being compressed into a small bead, pearl, crystal or pebble which you place into your satchel.

Now, once more, take a deep breath of air, focus upon opening your heart and focus upon what thing you would like to see manifested in your experience. What is something at the soul level that you would like to have or create? Tune into this object now. Feel, see, taste and experience the thing which you would like to see manifested and imagine its energy being compressed once again into a small crystal or pebble. Visualize it being compressed into a high-vibration seed or bead that you now place into your satchel or bag. Return your focus to the blank screen in front of you, within your mind, as you now tune into a quality that you would like to manifest in this next cycle of your life experience.

What quality are you tuning into now? What does it look like, feel like, and express itself like? What quality does your heart and soul guide you to want to manifest now? What quality of the Divine could you embrace in this next cycle of your life experience which would serve you and serve others and serve everything that is tuned into this quality now — to its energy, how it expresses itself, what it looks like and feels like. What is it? What quality?

Imagine the energy and the essence of this quality being compressed into a seed or crystal or pebble and energetically place this once again in your satchel.

At this time, tune into anything else which your heart is calling you to manifest, create or experience. Feel, understand and experience what this might be. What does it look like, feel like, taste like, sound like? Imagine the energy of it being compressed into a small seed or pebble or crystal which you now place into your satchel. And as you do this, the scene before your inner mind now shifts/ Imagine you're now standing on the banks of a Divine river of light. The stream of life-force energy flows before you. Hold your intentions, your satchel holding what you desire to be and create and experience in your right hand.

And when you are ready, pour out the contents of the satchel: your energetic beads, crystals, seeds or pebbles. Pour them into the stream, into the current of the river of life. They are now joining the stream of consciousness. Release your intentions into the light of the Divine and know that by remaining present in the moment, by remaining aware, you will be guided to the actions which you are required to take to align you with your desires and your intentions.

As the stream of life-force energy carries away your intentions, feel your attachment to the outcome releasing as well. Let go and let God. Trust in the process. Trust in your ability to create what you desire. And when you're ready, look and see, that gently flowing down the river of life is a raft specifically designed for you. Get on. Step in to the flow. Get into the river of life, the stream of consciousness, of Divine light, and flow with the course of events, flow into your future, into the next cycle, into your highest and greatest good. The Divine, the universe, everything is conspiring with you to manifest your dreams and intentions and your heart's desires. Among these are truths and beliefs.

Take action steps as you are intuitively guided. Knowing that you are meant to live vibrantly and excitedly however, wherever, and with whatever you want. And when you are in the flowing current of life, when you are in sync with the stream of consciousness, when you are in sync with All That Is, you attract the right people at the right time and the right circumstances and situations begin to manifest, to create, to make your dreams a reality.

You are now able to step into the light being that you really are from within the physical realm. . Allow your consciousness to return to your physical body, wherever you're now sitting or lying in in physical form. As you now receive in this place and state of consciousness, a final cleansing and uplifting, an alignment occurs with your highest and greatest good.

The full essence and energy of your higher self downloads now into your mind, body, spirit, into your emotions and your life energy. The knowledge and certainty and wisdom of your higher self linking with your being now so that you are able to, are willing to manifest your highest and greatest good in this new cycle of life which opens before you now, which begins now. All you must do is take the next step. The seeds have been planted, the intentions are set. The slate of the past is cleared and cleansed.

New frontiers, new horizons, uncharted territories open up before you. You are no longer confined by past limiting beliefs or doubts or fears. Release these and step forward into authentically, living as the Divine being in physical form that you are.

You are supported, blessed and uplifted. You are so loved and you are empowered. The time is now to take the reigns of control, to create and to bestow blessings. Plant the seeds of intention as they arise in your consciousness, as you have already done today. Focus on them, feel their essence and then release them over to the Divine to work hand in hand with you to make your dreams a reality, for your own benefit and for the well-being of all, for the highest and greatest good. And so it is.

I, Archangel Michael, now leave you with my blessing, with love and with the energy of well-being. I have empowered you to live vibrantly in alignment with your authentic truth and with your Divine self for the highest and greatest good. And so it is.

# Balance Self Love and Service

## ~Archangel Haniel

*D*earest one, indeed, I am Archangel Haniel and I am present here offering you the healing energy of the Divine. I offer you the well-being and the transformative power of love.

I invite you to relax as you read these words so that you also receive a Divine healing, uplifting your vibration and your frequency, the rate at which your very DNA vibrates. I speak to you now on balancing the nurturing energy that you direct towards yourself, and consciously taking action through love and service for others. The balance between these two flows of energy — love for self, and love for others — align you with the full and vibrant rounded-out purpose of your life.

Personal growth, evolution and forward advancement make it possible for you to positively impact the lives of others. Without personal growth as a foundation and building block, your service to others is limited because you will not have the required energy to invest. Nurturing yourself is a foundation which you can build upon to accomplish the greater extent of your life's work. Positively impacting this realm of the physical through simply being alive and being present and nurturing yourself advances you forward on your path of spiritual awakening and increased knowledge and understanding.

Learning and advancement creates a ripple far and wide of positivity that overflows into the lives of others. When you nurture yourself first, taking excellent care and treating yourself with vibrant love, you have the capacity and the energy and the willingness to actively and consciously provide guidance and service in the lives of others. And as your self-love and nurturing and personal growth creates a ripple throughout consciousness, your service to others, your kindness and shared love creates a tidal wave of positivity, of transformation, of healing light that flows throughout the universe and the greater field and realm of everything that is. It touches the lives of all subtly through the power of love, through vibration.

You are able to make a significant and lasting difference. At this time in this present, in this lifetime, there is no more waiting. Now is the time for action balanced with being, with personal reflection, connection with nature, being still, present, calm and reflective. The action steps will then appear and you will find yourself backtracking far less often, for your first step will be in the right direction.

With precision, laser focus, and inspired action, you are able to bring the blessings of the Divine into a physical form in your own life, at first energetically, consciously, with love and nurturing for yourself, beginning a great overflowing into the world that brings needed healing and light, uplifting and transformation here and now and for all time.

And so let yourself relax now and breathe deeply as raindrops of Divine healing, love and well-being pour down upon you and wash away the residue of past challenges, guilt and grief. Let the rain wash away past tensions and struggles and negativity, yours or others, conscious or unconscious, absorbed or remembered. Let go and let this Divine cleansing rain heal you, soothe you and bring rejuvenation to your being.

Imagine that this Divine rain is quickly filling your energetic reserves. It fills your bank of vitality and fills you with light. Your physical body, your mental, emotional, spiritual and auric energy — your light body — are filling with the light of the Divine so that you are now able to effortlessly overflow with Divine love, compassion, nurturing, well-being, excitement, gratitude and bliss. This is Divine love.

Now imagine that the raindrops from the Divine continue to pour into your being, turning into a steady flow of light. The faucet of Divine healing, of light and of well-being, is turned up so that light pours in at a constant stream. This is now accelerating your personal cleansing and uplifting, increasing your vibratory rate, assisting you in more effortlessly tuning into the guidance, healing and love of the Divine, the blessings of the universe, of Source, of All That Is. Let yourself feel, know and experience your oneness with the one life force energy flowing throughout the universe that makes up everything.

Feel and experience this oneness as you are continuously filled with light from the Divine. And now let yourself overflow so that you are consciously sending out blessings of well-being, of healing, of rejuvenation and of love into the lives of others. Kindness and service and compassion flow outwards from you, positively bestowing the blessings of the Divine on those around you, on those you know and on those you have not yet met, and on those you shall never meet but to whom you are connected nonetheless. They receive the blessing of Divine love through you from the Divine flow of light.

Breathe in deeply as light flows in, and as you exhale notice that the light flows out. You are a conduit, a channel of Divine light. And know that those whom you touch with kindness and compassion, with consideration, with a positive thought or blessing or intention, will create a ripple themselves. In this way, all are impacted by this simple exercise of uniting with the love of the Divine, the light and the healing and the well-being, and letting it overflow.

You are receiving nurturing, healing and guidance yourself first, making it possible for you to positively influence the lives of others. Receive, uplift, share and the ripple of transformation continues, soothing the burdens of past challenges and poor choices, empowering you with the knowledge that in this time and place you are supported, loved and assisted in living vibrantly, joyously, passionately, in living your authentic truth centered in Divine love connected to the Divine and to everything. Your life is positively transformed with love and abundance and well-being and bestowing this abundance unto all for the highest and greatest good, for all time, for all that is, for all that will be.

Breathe and feel the light still building around you, still vibrating quickly within and without. Carry this light throughout your life, for this is the most profound thing you can do to nurture yourself — to live with love and to carry light and love in your vibration. When you do this, you bring healing wherever you go. You bring positive transformation wherever you are. You bestow blessings to those around you by default, and all those whom you serve, the joy they connect with, the love, the success that they send out, returns to you multiplied.

The change which comes from within and is celebrated without, is positively empowered. By the light of the Divine, you are safe to change, to grow and to heal. You are loved, you are supported, all is well. Breathe in the light of the Divine. Let it fill you, uplift you, inspire you, and now as you exhale let the blessings of the Divine be bestowed upon all who you know, all whom you encounter, all whom you are connected with.

You are loved and empowered to consciously transform your life, to bring blessings into your own life by nurturing yourself, making it possible for you to positively impact others.

I, Archangel Haniel, leave you with a final surge of Divine healing, uplifting and inspiration. Breathe this in, let this in, radiate this, share this, live this, for it is your path, your right, your truth: to live with love, to inspire love, to heal with love, to know love and know that all is well.

As you continue forward, you will receive signs and signals and guidance that you are on your right path and how specifically you should continue. Love opens this guidance. Love opens the door. Act upon that which you receive and the door will open wider, letting more of your authentic truth shine into this present moment. This is needed. Now is the time. You are loved.

# 8

# Your Intuitive Guidance System

## ~ *Archangel Haniel*

*I*ndeed, I am Archangel Haniel. I invite you to breathe, to relax and to let go knowing that all is well in this moment — you are safe, you are surrounded by the love and healing energy of the Divine, and all is well.

Breathe freely as you relax, absorb the healing, nurturing and soothing energy of this moment. Breathe and relax your mind, relax your body, relax your energy. Enter into your open heart. Tune into the subtle vibrations of healing and Divine love which bring complete soothing and rejuvenation to you now mentally, physically, spiritually and emotionally.

Indeed, your feelings are balanced and purified, the feelings which serve you in so many ways. Your feelings act as an intuitive guidance system and when you honor them, you are able to perceive when you feel a bit off or when you feel upset or anxious about something. This can be a sign to move in another direction. Your feeling guidance system carries you further on your path of awakening as you follow your joys and passions and love. It moves you toward a more authentic connection with yourself and with Divine love.

This feeling guidance system operates best in the present moment. And as you feel in the present, in this moment, in direct response to what is happening now and intuitively foreseeing what will be, it can happen that your emotional guidance system can become bogged down. It happens when you are attuned to past feelings and dwell upon these past emotions and the vibrational energy signatures of sadness, of anxiety tied to past challenges and struggles of your present incarnation and of your past lifetimes.

And so to cleanse your emotional guidance system so that it will serve you now to determine whether your feeling is loving, is good, is validating your choice, or whether this feeling is bad, is painful, signifying that something is off, and that you would be served in moving in another direction.

In this moment you are able to determine the course that your feelings are plotting by asking first and foremost, *"Is this mine? Is this my feeling or am I empathically tuning into the feeling or vibration of another?"* This can be true if you are empathic and able to feel what another is feeling. Ask yourself, *"Is this mine?"* And if the feeling or emotion is indeed yours, ask, *"Is this tied to my present circumstances or is this tied to the past?"*

If it is tied to the past, let yourself feel the feeling and acknowledge it. Tell yourself *"I see this feeling, this feeling is mine."* And then release it. Feel the feeling and let it go. Return to a neutral state of being so that your feeling guidance system can encourage you to feel joy and things that are fulfilling, empowering, inspiring and that lead to health and vitality, so that bad feelings and challenging emotions don't appear, encouraging you to change your course.

*"Is this my feeling?"* is important to ask and when you do this, if you determine that no, it is not your feeling, take a deep breath and imagine a giant rose growing before you very close to your energy. This energetic rose is just outside your vibration and is using unconditional love to block out the feelings and emotions, tensions and struggles of others. Anything on your side of the rose is yours. In this way you're able to filter out the storm of energies belonging to others so that you can in the present moment tune into what is yours and what is real.

And this brings us to a final question: *"Is this true?"* Whenever you are feeling a painful emotion and you are challenged by your feeling ask: "Is this true"?

Feelings can be triggered by your mind as well as by your intuition. Asking *"Is this true?"* is the same as asking *"Is this in response to something that is happening in my reality now or is this in response to a fear or scenario that is playing out in my ego and causing me to feel bad? Is this feeling mine? Is this feeling real and true? Is this feeling tied to my present scenario?"*

Utilize these questions to harness the power of your feelings. This becomes a mechanism for validating your intuition and for aligning your path to a clearer knowledge of the direction in which lies your highest and greatest good. Utilizing your emotional guidance system works best in a neutral state and so let us go now through the process once more of releasing the challenging feelings from the past.

Focus inward as you read, breathing freely, knowing you are supported, and tuning in to a feeling from the past which does not serve your highest good. What feeling has been repressed and yet is still stored in your cellular memory, in your emotional being, in your mental, emotional or spiritual body?

Tune into this feeling now. Acknowledge the feeling that comes up: "*I see you*".

Let yourself feel whatever this feeling is. Acknowledge it as yours whether it is tied to the present moment, to past scenarios or even to past lives. Feel the feeling and let it go.

"*I release you over to the angels now and into the light for the highest and greatest good, with love and compassion.*" This process returns you to a more neutral state of being aware, being present and centered, able to release more painful feelings if needed, to return to neutrality, and with this awareness you are able to be guided by your feeling away from what is painful or challenging or tense and towards what is free, what is true, what is love, and what serves your highest and greatest good.

At this time, breathe freely as a waterfall of light flows around you, cleansing your mind, body and spirit. It assists you in becoming centered, present and aware, ready to observe and respond to the situations of your life, to the upcoming choices, obstacles and challenges.

Take note of how you feel now, and moving forward follow the path of joy and love to your highest good.

I, Archangel Haniel, leave you with my blessing and with Divine light and endless love.

# 9

# Rejuvenation
# Meditation

## ~ *Archangel Muriel*

Greetings, dear one. I am Archangel Muriel, present with you here and now. Once again you are at the point of a powerful new beginning. It is the dawning of a new day. Doors are opening for you. You are empowered to co-create with the Divine what you want and need — what will serve you in moving forward.

Understand that this service of the self is in alignment with your ability to serve others. You are moving forward now, loving, nurturing and rejuvenating your being, your Self, your soul, your mind, body and spirit with the light of the Divine. You are setting new intentions concerning things which you want to experience, which you need to experience and which will serve you in living in joy and harmony and love. Moving forward and through this alignment with Divine love, you are able to overflow your gratitude, love and blessings unto all.

And so while you are serving your Self in the short-term, in the grand scheme and in the greater picture this personal alignment with Divine love, this re-energizing, healing and rejuvenation of yourself which you are stepping into now is a prerequisite and a step on your greater path of offering magnificent service to all consciousness, beings, life and All That Is. For your positive energy sphere, your state of being, your thoughts, your emotions, your energy and your actions create a ripple of light throughout everything.

Know that you are supported now in rejuvenating your being, in healing, and in tapping into the energy of renewal so that you have the energy, the motivation and the ambition to make your dreams a reality as you step into this new cycle of creation, this new cycle of being focused and manifesting what you need, want and desire.

And so at this time, let yourself focus inward. Open your heart and look within. Breathe and relax. Relax your feet and your toes. Relax your legs, your calves and your thighs. Relax your knees. Relax your hips. Relax your buttocks, your abdomen and your lower back. Breathe and relax your upper back, your chest, your shoulders, arms and hands.

As you read, breathe and relax your neck, your jaw, your ears, your chin, your forehead. Relax your eyes, relax your entire head. Breathe, let go of tension, and relax. At this time, physically tense your body slightly and then relax even deeper.

Let go of thoughts as they appear, simply focusing inward. Breathe, relax and read these words as you let go.

In just a moment you're going to be transported consciously through your imagination and through your conscious awareness to a beautiful ocean shore. This is possible as you read through your minds eye, or you may wish to read the experience once, and then repeat the meditative exercise again with your eyes closed.

Take a deep breath. Imagine that an orb of light surrounds you and in the count of 3, 2, 1 you're magically transported to the seaside, to a beautiful ocean shore where you find a comfortable place to sit, consciously visualizing and tuning into this visualization.

Imagine you're sitting on the beach listening to the ocean waves gently lapping against the shore. Relax and breathe. Feel the energy of the sand beneath you. Notice the energy of the plants and trees around you. Hear the birds in the distance and the sound of the waves moving in your direction. Notice the water, which is connected to All That Is and connected to the Divine. Water radiates light, renewal and rejuvenation. Be aware of these healing properties of the water which is before you now.

As the next wave rolls toward the shore, consciously visualize the energetic field of this wave, the energy of the water continuing forward and washing over you in a gentle stream. Let it cleanse your being. As this happens, as your energy merges with the subtle energy of the water, let go, relax and let the water wash away tension, stress and past challenges.

As another wave of the ocean of light before you surges forward, feel the energy of the water. Feel this ocean of light washing over you, washing away addictions, past choices which do not serve, and past patterns which are not in alignment with what you really want and need and desire.

Let go. Release these vibration patterns, these energies which do not serve. Let the energy of the ocean carry these lower-vibration patterns away. Another surge comes forward, a wave approaches the shore, and the energy of the light, of the Divine, of the ocean, of water washes over your being rejuvenating your mind, body and spirit. It brings the energy of renewal, of vitality and of healing into your being at this present point and time.

Breathe it in. Let your subtle energy merge with the subtle energy of renewal and the healing properties of water, and let go. As another wave approaches the shore, feel the subtle energy of the ocean of light before you washing over your being. Relax and let go. As this ebb and flow of the ocean's energy continues and brings the healing and rejuvenating energy into your being, let the energy of renewal fill you. Let this healing and rejuvenating energy fill your entire being, uplifting you, cleansing you, energizing and renewing you. Let it prepare you for this new cycle, for your new beginning.

As you simply relax and delight in the energy of the Divine, represented as this ocean of light, the waves crash on the shore and the subtle energy of the water washes over you, cleansing, renewing and healing your being.

Imagine holding your hands out before you and see in your minds eye that you hold two stones, one in each hand. You hold a black stone in your left hand and a white stone in your right one. The black stone represents what you're ready to move on from: dense energy from your past, addictions or habits or patterns or processes which do not serve you and that you're ready to let go of. The white stone in your right hand represents your future, your potential, your unlimited possibilities which lie before you. It contains the essence of what you want and need, of what is inspiring and rewarding and empowering for you as you move forward.

Take a deep breath and use your left hand to throw the black stone into the ocean of light. Release these old patterns, release tensions and dense energy, release the past, let go of it, let it be in the past, let it dissolve into the ocean of light so that you can move on. Now tune into the infinite possibility before you. Take the stone in your right hand and throw it into the ocean of light as well. Release your attachment to any outcome, surrender your goals and dreams and aspirations to the Divine.

Now you have effectively released what has been, and you have released what could be, and in this moment you are simply connected to what is, connected to the ocean of light before you, to the Divine presence that runs throughout everything, which reminds you that anything is possible, that you can co-create what you want and need and desire.

And once more as a wave crashes upon the shore, feel the energy of the Divine, the rejuvenating energy of water from the ocean of light before you surging over your being. It cleanses, heals, rejuvenates and renews your being so that you have the energy, the motivation and the ambition to make your dreams, needs, wants and desires a reality.

You can make a huge difference in this world beginning by creating what you want and need and then moving into serving and loving and overflowing the blessings of the Divine to others.

Take another moment to simply sit here in awareness, feeling the energy of the Divine presence in the ocean of light before you washing over your being, rejuvenating your mind, body and spirit, mixing with your subtle energy, reminding you that you are one with the Divine, one with the light, and one with All That Is.

Through this oneness you are able to co-create what you most desire. Let yourself tune into your intentions for this next cycle of being. Tune into the knowledge of what you want to experience, what you need to create, what will serve you moving forward. Open your heart and let this knowledge be impressed upon your consciousness directly from your heart and soul and higher self.

And now, rejuvenated, newly focused and present, let yourself return consciously to your physical body and the present point in time, to the point of infinite possibility. You are now uplifted, cleansed and energized and ready to make a difference in your life and in the greater universe. You are ready, you are loved and supported. I am Archangel Muriel and I leave you with my blessing.

# 10

# Mastery of Love

## ~ *Orion*

Greetings, indeed, I am Orion. I am present with you now and greet you in this moment of Divine frequency which serves to activate your inner light, to activate your Christ light, your Christ consciousness, cosmic consciousness, your higher consciousness.

Simply breathe freely and relax as Divine light and uplifted frequency enters into your present space and time. Feel and be aware of the Divine light all around you. Let yourself open your inner eyes to see, your inner senses to feel and know, your Christ consciousness to increase your awareness beyond the confines of the physical world peering in, stepping in, lifting up to experience the higher realms of spirit.

As you open your heart, as you embrace loving choices and actions towards yourself and others, as you walk this path of love in the present moment, the increased levels of Divine light frequency merge together and align with your being. The realms of higher consciousness and possibility open up before you to experience as you are right now, in your blissful, peaceful state of being. This is the experience of the higher realms: tranquil, loving, Divine.

Breathe and lift higher, breathing in the white light that is all around, which cleanses your being, which uplifts your vibration, which enables you to tune into the presence of your team of guides and angels around you always, present within.

Lift and be aware, with your psychic sight and with your subtle senses, through your Christ light of the Divine presence, the presence of Divine love, and the presence of Divine beings who love you dearly, who are here to assist you on your path of awakening and unfolding, of uplifting and experiencing the higher realms in your meditation, and throughout your life.

Be alert, aware and present in the moment, able to handle your worldly responsibilities, able to play the game of life in the most physical sense. You are able to master these games of survival, of money, of relationships, of love, of work and service, of physical well-being and vitality while simultaneously mastering the game of the spiritual dimension. For indeed, there are multiple dimensions simultaneously interwoven into this present moment and as you access the spiritual frequencies and light, you are accessing alternate dimensions of the Divine presence, accessible from your physical reality, and yet existing on an entirely different wavelength.

This is an exciting time in which you live, in which the dimensions are merging, the light of angels and the wisdom of interdimensional beings and guides and the love of the ascended masters who exist in another realm are able to be profoundly felt and experienced by you in your life. The qualities of these beings of light — archangels, ascended masters and your spirit guides of the light — are able to be infused into your being. You are able to feel and know and experience the qualities of your higher self, which is fully connected to the Divine at all times.

And as you live, as an awakened spiritual being in the present moment, a master of the physical and spiritual aspects of life, you gain alignment with your Christ light and with the mastery of Love.

Love opens doors and lays foundations, it paves pathways into new possibilities. Love activates and inspires. It unlocks the doors to your abilities and gifts and latent talents. Love heals the physical, mental, emotional and spiritual being.

Love heals relationships and challenging situations, soothes tensions, eases burdens, and by this I speak not of platonic love or romantic love or self-love. I speak of Love with a capital L. I speak of Divine love which is unconditional, irrevocable, ever-present and waiting for you. Lift up and tune into it. Channel Love's blessings through you and live Love with your heart awakened, your mind focused, your spiritual being infused with the blessings of the Divine. Let the blessings of Love flow through your life opening doors, aligning meetings, working with the law of attraction and the law of synchronicity.

At this time I, Orion, and your teams of guides and angels direct the energy of this Divine love your way. We bestow this unconditional love upon you to illuminate your being, cleanse your energy, soothe your tensions and burdens, and simply allow you in this moment to experience what it feels like, to know you are infinitely loved by the Divine, by the universe, by All That Is.

See the blessings of Love flowing throughout your life. Understand the ripple of positive energy that is initiated by each choice you make that is aligned with Love. Know and experience Love for yourself and Love for all.

Love is your master path, your accelerated path of ascension toward elevating your vibration, and progressing in the direction of growth. This growth is personally, consciously, spiritually and Divinely aligning with your highest possible potentials for this life, your highest and greatest good, and the way in which you may most vibrantly live and love and serve and make a difference.

Divine love is all around you. Breathe it in, feel it flow throughout your being, rejuvenating your energy, healing you at the cellular level and at the mental level, and at the spiritual level, aligning new creative ideas, new possibilities and new perspectives.

An orb of white light and rose-colored light glows around you. This is the energy of Divine and unconditional love. This light works to filter out all that is not love, releasing it into the light. This light also serves to help you see the Divine love that is always present, to see the silver lining, the hidden blessing, the unnoticed benefit, the positive attribute, the Love in whatever you're currently experiencing or going through or being tested with, or learning about.

By choosing to respond with Love and by looking for the Love that is present, by directing Love towards the situation, obstacles are removed and blockages are released. You can make it through anything by leveraging the power of Love.

And you are supported in this, you are applauded as you continue on this path of loving fully, vibrantly, wholly all of life, loving all, which aligns Love's blessing throughout all and directs it back to you.

As a quick exercise and example, breathe in the white- and rose-colored light of Love that is all around you so that you are filled with Love from within. Now imagine that you're sending Love out to the earth, to All That Is, directing your Love out in gratitude and thanks and compassion, these facets in the intricately cut diamond that is Love.

Direct love outward, and now witness and feel the love returned to you multiplied as all of life responds with joy, with love, with compassion, returning Love back to you tenfold.

Breathe it in, let it fill you, let it enter into this present point of time, and now ground all of this Love to the earth, into your life now, feeling light flowing down through the bottom of your feet, anchoring you to the earth. Feeling the light at the earth's core flow up through all of your *chakras*, up out the top of your head, up as high as you can think and imagine and visualize, anchoring you to the Divine, to the universe, and to infinite possibility above.

And these two lights from below and from above, flow up and flow down, and unite in your center, in your open heart, creating a burst of Love which expands outward and infuses your paradigm and your life with the infinite possibilities made accessible through Love for the highest and greatest good.

I, Orion, leave you with my Love. Your guides and angels direct Love and all of creation sends Love your way. Breathe it in, release it out. This is a cycle of giving and receiving Love which paves your pathway, which accelerates your growth, which lifts your vibration, which serves you and serves all. This is your path of stepping fully into your Christ light of awakened living.

You have become a Christ-conscious being through the path of Love, through your open heart, and through your intricate connection to all. Love and know that you are so loved in return.

# 11

# Dimensional Hopping

## ~ *Archangel Metatron*

*G*reetings, dearest one. Indeed, I am Archangel Metatron. I am pleased to connect with you at this point in time, in this present moment, when you are able to access infinite realities and alternate dimensions. Infinite possibilities are available to you now within this present moment.

Understand that your dreams, your desires, your goals and the characteristics you wish to embody more fully have already manifested in the alternate dimensions. There is already an aspect of yourself who is a master of the current skills you are working to learn, and who is already living the dream or intention you desire.

You live in a universe of infinite possibilities and unlimited parallel dimensions and realities. We bring you this information now for you are able to dimension hop to integrate qualities of your alternate self that you wish to embody in this present expression and experience.

You are able to connect with the wealth and confidence, the psychic ability or joy of your alternate self, experiencing the reality of those characteristics, and embracing energetically and consciously the attributes, experiences, and manifestations you desire now. You do this by attuning yourself to the alternate reality where this is already present. You are able to draw yourself closer to this now. You are able to energetically align yourself with that possibility for the purpose of manifesting what you desire and, in many cases, realizing that you already have what you need to draw toward you — that which you seek right now already is in other line of time. We will walk you through this process, for you have this ability and a direct connection.

You see, you live in a time when the veil between the physical and spiritual realms is thin, a time in which the veil between your present dimensional experience and the limitless alternate realities and dimensions is able to be passed through. They dimensions are tied together and all are occurring simultaneously in this present moment.

Your spirit is focused on this present reality, but as you become more energetically sensitive, alternate realities subtly slip in and you become aware that you are perceiving what is happening in this experience and in all others. You are able to become aware of your full multidimensional self.

And so to begin to attune yourself to characteristics that you desire, relax. Breathe freely and let your mind be still and calm, let your body relax. Allow your spiritual being to be activated.

Know that when you consciously relax, your body allows healing vibrations in. When you consciously relax, your spirit awakens, opens and attunes you to the spiritual realms. And so relax and breathe freely and open your heart. Imagine that you are standing in a circle of light — a three dimensional orb of golden, white light. Imagine that you are at the center of your sun, which is a portal or vortex to alternate dimensions and realities.

Being present in this circle, within this sun, you are then able to transport yourself consciously to any dimensional experience you choose.

What quality do you wish to more fully embody? What characteristic in the expansive catalog of possibilities of the universe do you wish to embody? Breathe and plant this seed of thought in your consciousness now.

Whether it is vibrant health, new levels of abundance, more confidence, clarity or connection, plant the seed of thought now about the quality or characteristic you desire, and then we are going to count you back from 3 to 1, at which point you will energetically and consciously be transported to the dimension, to the reality, to the knowing and ability to perceive and meet the aspect of yourself that has already mastered this quality, that is living in full alignment with that which you desire.

Relax and as you read once again notice the Divine, golden light orb all around you, the light of the sun all around you. Breathe in the light, relax and feel your frequency elevate as you relax and as your body attunes to the healing vibrations of the Divine.

Breathe freely and in 3, 2, 1 imagine that you're transported into a dimension in which you fully embody these gifts of the Divine, in which you fully embody the qualities and characteristics you desire now.

Let your imagination be activated.

Begin to paint a mental picture of what this looks like, of what illumination of your gifts means. How has the quality you desire manifested in this alternate dimension you're tuning into.

Notice the qualities and characteristics that appear. Notice your surroundings. What is different from your current life and what is the same?

Notice your energetic being, your emotional state, notice your physical and spiritual connections. Be aware. Using your intuitive, imaginative gift, notice all the possibilities that open up from your aligning with this attribute you carry in a parallel dimension.

Notice how this attribute has manifested in this alternate dimension you are experiencing and perceiving now. Let all your subtle senses be engaged to clairvoyantly see the scene, hear the sounds, smell, notice, perceive and grow aware of this attribute fully manifested in yourself in this alternate dimension.

Be aware, that you are tuning into and viewing this parallel existence from above, from an outside perspective. But as you notice this you begin to draw closer, bringing yourself into alignment with the scene you are painting with your imagination and your intuition, bringing the quality into alignment with your being now, consciously, through the power of awareness.

Feel yourself merge with this alternate dimensional self. Integrate the quality into your energetic and spiritual being. Align yourself with the dreams, the characteristics and circumstances you desire in your present life. Experience energetically what it feels like to bring about this manifestation. Experience the blessing of that which you desire. See the scene around you. Know the blessings and benefits of this quality. Experience already having it, for, again, this alternate dimension is real. Any possibility you can perceive is manifesting on an alternate plane, and when you consciously transport yourself there through the vortex of the sun, you can effortlessly experience being in it and experience the validity of it, the truth of it, the realness of it.

And when you do this, you are consciously aligning with it and bringing your current physical, mental, emotional and spiritual being into alignment with this alternate aspect of you that already has what you desire.

Breathe and relax. Feel yourself merge with the gifts of your alternate self. Feel yourself letting go of any perceived struggle that is normally required to create what you want, any doubt that you're not able to do it, any doubt that you don't deserve it, and realign with the knowledge that in this present moment, it already is manifest.

What does that feel like to know you have what you want? To have what you desire? To have what you need? Experience this, let it enter into your emotional and mental being. Become aware that you are closely aligning with what you desire.

You are able to repeat this process and transport yourself so that you integrate all the qualities that you seek, all the conscious desires that you would like to see in your life.

We'll now count you back from 3 to 1, at which point you'll be present and aware once again in your current life and reality, more closely aligned to the goals you desire, the characteristics you seek, and with a new found knowledge that you are able to manifest anything that you want, for energetically it already exists and, indeed, you live in a realm of infinite possibility.

And with this new belief, all things — emotional, conscious, mental, physical and spiritual, and all actions, anything, everything, is possible for you.

So in 3, 2, 1...

Through the portal of the sun, you now return fully and consciously in an orb of light to your present reality, to your present life. This orb of light remains around you and cleanses any doubt that you have. It releases any fear and uncertainty. It reminds you energetically and mentally that you can and you will succeed. All things are possible.

What is your next step? What is your action to take to complete this link, this merging, and to bring yourself as you are in your present physical reality into alignment with what you seek?

The energetic pathway has been laid, and the field of consciousness has been rearranged, so act upon your intuitive nudges, take action, have faith, trust, and draw the blessings you desire into your being.

Consciously relax, for when you relax, healing and light are able to effortlessly flow throughout your body. Breathe in the light that is all around you and as you breathe out, let it flow through your entire being. Any trapped energy dissipates and dissolves. Breathe in new, fresh light, and as you breathe out, let it once again cycle through your entire being, improving your life continually every day in every way.

You are getting better and better. You're improving and moving into closer alignment with your dreams and goals. Once you pave the energetic pathway, the manifestation process has begun.

Stay focused on what you desire, take the action steps you are able to take, release attachment to what is now and to what will be, and what you desire is now able to enter in, and to be created for you to experience now in this life, in this body, in this present time.

Beloved one, I, Archangel Metatron, leave you now with a final surge of light, uplifting your energy, activating all your *chakras*, cleansing, purifying and activating your light.

Shine brightly, for with love, with joy, with passion and compassion you draw unto you blessings, gifts and that which you desire. You can and you will, for now I am complete.

# 12

# Your Soul Ascension

## ~ *Archangel Michael*

*B* eloved one! Indeed, I, Archangel Michael, am present and greet you now. Accept the light of the Divine surrounding you, cleansing you. It assists you in ascending by releasing what no longer serves, by integrating new levels of Divine spirit into your being.

What have you been carrying throughout your life? Carrying throughout your days? Carrying from your time of birth? Carrying with you from lifetimes past along the journey of your soul?

What feelings, energies and frequencies are you experiencing, are you using to create? What energy are you carrying within your vibrational being?

Ascension is not only lifting into the light and integrating the Divine into your being. That is true in part, but your ascension is also cleansing and purifying your soul so that you may more purely align with the Divine in oneness, in love, and in radiant well-being.

In this present lifetime and in your lifetimes past, each of your experiences contains an energy. Your joys and triumphs, your deepest, darkest secrets and regrets, are energetically managed and stored in your soul's records.

Your soul is the vibrational being that you are, that exists here and now in the physical realm, in your body in physical form, but which also spans time and exists simultaneously in multiple dimensions outside of time and space. Your soul contains the essence of your past and future and present selves. All your past and future and present vibrations and energies, are each contained within you, within your soul, as energy.

This is why you walk the ascension path: to cleanse and purify the trauma and hardship and density still contained within your soul's sphere of energy. This is passed on ancestrally, passed on through your mother during birth, passed on through learning and media signals and experiences of your life gathered throughout lifetimes, and throughout present momenta. Your soul's sphere of energy is created in response to things you experience, choices you make, and to energy and vibration.

And so your soul contains the record of all that you are and all you have been, and you are empowered through this fullness now.

This is a time of accelerated being and more light is available. The veils of illusion between you and the Divine are thinned. They have become nonexistent at certain points and places so that you, your soul and physical being are able to link directly with the Divine light. You are able to enlighten your soul, raise it and your physical being's vibration, and become Divinity manifest and expressed through you.

At this time, you are surrounded with Divine cleansing

light, guided by the Divine and guided by your team of guides and angels who direct this light your way in order to cleanse that which you are still carrying and which no longer serves.

Let go, release, cleanse your being, your body and soul of density, tragedy, negativity, tension, stress, fear and doubt. Imagine that a column of white light is now placed around you acting as a Divine vacuum at the top of your head pulling out the negative thoughts, energies and vibrations which are weighing you down. Release and let go.

As this happens you lift upward and now a waterfall of Divine light pours down around you to fill the void you've left. It fills your soul with love, with compassion, with Divine attributes of peace, harmony and connection. It fills your mind, body and spirit with light of high-vibration, with unconditional love from the Divine.

Accept this energy! Imagine you're pulling this Divine energy into your being, lifting you up as you draw the Divine light down, integrating light into your soul and spirit, into your body and mind, into your emotions, into your thought forms, aligning you with the Divine being you are able to manifest as now, aligning you with your inner radiant spirit that is your authentic state of being, that is the you that exists outside of the physical realms, outside of density and duality, in oneness with source at all times.

This higher presence merges with your soul being now to cleanse, uplift and purify it, aligning it with total Divine love.

This work paves the path, but you must be and are an active participant in your ascension journey. You choose your thoughts, what to accept, what to believe and what to create. This is your choice in the present moment — your choice of love or fear, your choice of doubt or belief, your choice of darkness or light.

You are in the realm of duality still. Your soul has much experience in this density and in the cleansing of wounds from past lessons and challenges and obstacles. Know that as you do this work, as you let go of those old thoughts, old feelings and of those old beliefs, you are able to choose anew. You're able to choose consciousness, awareness, presence, clarity, and love.

Let your love grow. Let your soul, your body, your mind, your emotions and your spirit be cleansed and uplifted. Choose to be present and to be aware. Choose whether you engage your ego or whether you engage your inner spirit, and your Divine light. This is your choice in this moment, this is your ascension path. This is your classroom of life, this is your opportunity now.

Divine light, which cleanses, uplifts and inspires you now, is always available. Your higher self and spirit, remember that part of you that existed before birth and will continue after death, outside of time and space, which is one with the Divine, one with everything, one with source, God, all that is existing without any separation in complete and Divine love. This higher Divine self can be aligned into your being for total clarity, presence, illumination, enlightenment, ascension and love.

Feel this alignment as your higher Self merges with your soul, with your physical being, with you here and now in this present moment. This link is empowering your choice, empowering your path, and illuminating the path of love before you. Yes, there still exists density in your realm. Yes, there are obstacles and hurdles and challenges you must work through. But returning to love and to living as the embodiment of Divine spirit, you will glide effortlessly through. Return to love, return to Divine presence, return to linking through your open heart and lifting into the realms above to combine with All That Is.

In direct connection with Source, with All That Is, with the Divine, you can call in your guides, your support team who will assist you in cleansing and purifying further, in guiding and uplifting further, in empowering you further to live as the full embodiment of Divine light in the physical realm. Live in alignment with the Divine attributes, and with your higher spirit to transcend duality, to live in Love.

Your team of guides, angels, ascended masters and ancestors direct their love and blessing toward you now. They send a final surge of energy to cleanse and purify you, to align you with the willingness, with the knowingness that you are able to choose this enlightened perspective, this ascended state of being, this oneness with the Divine and with All That Is.

Imagine all this energy now gathering in your center, flowing down and grounding to the earth and to All That Is. Your choice is in the present moment. Your choice appears with every step you take. Your choice is now. Choose wisely. Choose Love.

# 13

# Connecting With Your Ascension Team

## ~ *Archangel Michael*

*G*reetings, indeed, I am Archangel Michael, present here and now with you and your team of guides and angels of Divine light. We surround you with healing and tranquil energy of the Divine to uplift, to renew, and to inspire.

In this moment and in every moment, you are able to link directly with the Divine and through this direct connection with the Divine, with All That Is, you are then able to focus the conscious connection to make the link with your angels and, indeed, with your ascended masters.

Indeed, you can link now with fairies and spirit guides and even your loved ones who exist beyond the veil.

There are processes by which you are able to link with these guides and beings and loved ones without directly linking with the Divine first. But as you are an ascending being, as you are a being who is walking the path of love and living life with an increased vibration, you are advised to make the connection first with All That Is and with the Divine and then to connect with the various realms of spirit, planes of existence, and parallel dimensions according to Divine will for the highest and greatest good.

When you proceed forward in this way, the benefits of the many realms and dimensions beyond the physical become accessible while bypassing the need to experience the duality, mischief or resistance. You no longer need to take on any sort of lower vibration and you remain able to tune into any benefits for you, any lessons, teachings, love, guidance or insights available therein.

This is a process you can use to connect with your angels for guidance and with your ancestors and loved ones, your spirit guides and the ascended masters. It can also be used to tune into the records held within crystals, the healing properties of crystals and stones and earth objects, to tune into and to telepathically connect with animals, your power animals, your spirit animals who hold healing powers and insight for you at this moment and forever. You can connect without detriment through the lens of All That Is by linking first with Source, with the Divine, with all.

And this process is simple. As you focus inward and relax, imagine that you are surrounded by a pure white light of Divine nature which surrounds you completely and totally in this dimension and in others. This white light of the Divine lifts you up and cleanses you, and protects your energy. By your simply thinking of having white light all around you, you call it in. Breathe in the white light and as you exhale, relax and let go.

Enter into this present moment, become aware of your breathing, aware of the light which is all around you and within you. Breathe in the white light, exhale while letting go of tensions, worries, frustrations and doubts.

Breathe in one more time, and now as you exhale imagine your energy flowing downward, grounding you to the core of the earth, grounding you to the light at the earth's core, flowing way down until you are connected with a beautiful light therein, the light at the soul level of earth which is connected to the Divine, which is connected with you, which is connected to All That Is.

Experience your oneness with this light at the earth's core, your oneness with the earth, your oneness with everything and now let the light flow upward.

The white and golden light is interwoven together in a beautiful braid that flows up through your feet, up your spinal column, traveling upward and cleansing and elevating your vibration, magnetizing your personal power, your presence and your focus in this very place and time. Flowing up out your crown, out of the top of your head, above your upper *chakras*, above the lights, above the angelic realm, above the realms of ascended masters, above the spiritual planes, up as high as you can imagine, up into the light, into the direct presence with Source and with All That Is.

Go up, way up, lift into the light, into the direct presence with Source, God, the one life-force energy flowing throughout everything, and that you are a part of. Feel your oneness with this, your oneness with the Divine, your oneness with all of life, your oneness with All That Is. Breathe and be aware.

Let go and just be here now in this space which elevates your vibration. Just be here now in this presence with the Divine which illuminates your spirit, which rejuvenates your being, which cleanses, and which elevates your frequency through your awareness, oneness, connection, with the light of the Divine, and with All That Is. And from within this space, from within this energy at this present point in time you may think or say, *"I now invite my highest, best, most loving possible angel who can most serve me now. Please come in and connect with me now according to Divine will."*

Open your heart, open up your energy. Allow the earth energy below to flow up through your open heart and up into your higher energetic centers. Allow the light of the Divine essence and the light of your angel who can best serve you now — let it flow down through your crown to a *chakra* at the back of your head, through your throat and through your heart.

Feel, know and experience the presence of your angel with you here and now. Notice the presence of your angel who vibrates with a specific energy pattern. It is an energy signature so that you can recognize their presence moving forward.

Be aware of how you feel now, of what you see now, of what you hear, of what you smell. Pay attention to your subtle psychic senses as your angel, the one who can most serve you, unites with you in this present moment. Notice your feeling, your state of being, and the mental images, thoughts and impressions which appear in your consciousness, which deliver the guidance of your angel to you now.

Take a moment to pause and close your eyes. Breathe and receive that which will most serve you now from your angel according to Divine will.

A message, an energy, a symbol and token of their guidance, support and love. Receive the symbol from your angel. And now if you would like you may ask a question in the mind of your angel who will best serve you now. Or you may set the intention, *"Please help me with this aspect of my life. Or help me tune into whatever will most serve me now."* Receive as you simply breathe and become aware of the guidance of your angel now.

Express your gratitude for this being of light who has shown up for you today. And now as they step back, you may feel a wave of love and then notice the subtle difference as you return to simply being aware of your oneness with the Divine, through your connection to All That Is.

Realign yourself, lift up into the light, merge with Source, embrace life, combine with All.

At this time the ascended master who can best serve you now, the spirit guide who has walked upon this earth and who has mastered the game of life, who guides you from spirit as an ascended and awakened being, will this master please step forward now to merge with your being, to make their presence known to you so that you can experience them now and know when they are with you?

As your ascended master guide steps forward, this is the guide who can best help you now as you continue your journey of ascension, as you walk a path of life mastery. This guide, this ascended being is here to help, to guide, to love and to assist you. Notice their presence. Be aware of their unique energy signature. Observe the connection you have with this being.

How does it feel? Where do you experience the presence of this ascended one? What do you see, hear and smell with your subtle senses?

What message do you receive as your ascended guide shares with you whatever it is that will most serve you now?

Receive the message which may be audibly understood in words or may simply be a frequency for you to feel and experience. Receive the insight and wisdom of your guide who has mastered physical life on earth and who now guides you from the other side as an ascended being, as a master of light who excitedly awaits you to join in the circle of light of ascended beings, to claim your seat and assume your place after your graduation from life and your full ascension into the realm of spirit.

Receive the energy, blessing and love of your guide who is an ascended being and who steps forward for you now. Take another moment to energetically commune with your guide and receive their love and blessing.

And as they now step back into the light, you may notice a final surge of their love and gratitude.

Let your gratitude flow in return. Return your focus, your present moment awareness to your direct link with the Divine, God, and All That Is. Be aware of this connection and with the healing, cleansing and uplifting properties you are uniting with through this connection.

And from this place, at this time, in the direct presence of Source and aware of your connection with all of life, with everything that is, your totem power animal steps forward now or flies forward or swims forward.

Notice the presence of your power animal — the one who can best help you now with your current lessons and objectives in life. Feel, see, experience and receive a mental image of what your power animal is.Feel their presence, notice where you feel your connection with your power animal. How does this feel and differ from the angel and ascended master guide?

Be aware of the presence of your power animal who offers you their gift and blessing which will most serve you now.

Receive the blessing of your power animal and as they step back into the light, into direct presence with Source and with All That Is, feel the final surge of their support and their energy backing you.

Give thanks and return your focus back to your connection to the Divine, and from this place of connection to Source and to All That Is, become aware of the mineral or crystal which is serving you now, the one which can best serve and assist you through increasing consciousness and providing support.

Whether or not you possess a physical representation of this stone or mineral, the support is there. Tune into this crystal, mineral or element now.

This living consciousness will serve you and is connected to everything that is, just as you are.

Be aware of how your connection with this element or mineral feels. What do you see that represents this? What insight or energetic support is available for you from it?

Receive the blessing and now shift your focus back to the awareness of your connection with God and with All That Is. Breathe freely and enjoy paying attention to your breathing and being aware of your connection with everything, being aware of your oneness with God, with the Divine, with Source, with All That Is.

At this moment your *elemental* or fairy or *diva* guide steps forward. This is an energetic being who can help you work with the earth elements and tap into the benefits of your connection with the earth. This being who offers support and wisdom and blessings for you now, who can serve best according to Divine will, steps forward to connect with you now.

Experience your connection with your *elemental* or fairy or nature spirit guide. What do they look like? Feel like? And what message or frequency or pattern of energy do they direct your way?

Receive this — it will serve you best on your path as a seeker of truth, as a Divine being connected to all that is present on earth in physical form.

As this beloved being steps back into the light, return your focus to your direct connection with the Divine. The Divine cleanses and uplifts, soothes and balances, and aligns blessings on your path. It inspires creative possibilities and potentials, heals, soothes and rejuvenates.

In direct presence with Source, with God, with All That Is, your beloved ancestor in the realm of spirit steps forward. Your ancestor has a message for you. Your beloved ancestor who loves you and watches over you from the other side, steps forward now according to Divine will.

Experience your connection with this loved one through the lens of your oneness with the Divine and with everything. How do you experience the presence of your ancestor or loved one who is here with you now? What message or energy do they offer your way?

Thank them for showing up for you today and when your loved one or ancestor steps back into the light, return your focus to your connection with the Divine and with All That Is.

And finally in this place, through the lens of your direct connection with Source, the full presence of your higher self aligns with your physical being in this present moment. The full ascended version of you aligns with you in this present moment, uplifting you and blessing you.

The higher presence of you offers key insights necessary for your path and purpose. These enter into your awareness and align with your being according to Divine will for the highest and greatest good. And so it is.

Open your heart, thank your higher self. Feel your connection to the Divine and to All That Is. And now imagine all of this light pouring down in through your upper *chakras*, through your crown, through your third eye, throat and heart. It descends to your solar plexus, sacrum and root. It flows down through your legs once again to the earth, to the light at the earth's core which you are a part of and which is a part of All That Is.

And now pull the light up once more. Bring it to your open heart. In this moment, feel your power. Feel all the blessings you've received from all your guides in all their many shapes and forms and sizes who love you dearly.

Feel this personal power returning to you, returning to your center. It gathers in this present moment, in your present state of being.

This power which has been lost or left behind in past experiences. The energy which has been drained, consciously or unconsciously, by other persons or activities. All of your power, all of your energy returns to you now to your center, energizing your life, illuminating your path, inspiring you to live authentically and true to the unique and Divine spiritual being that you are.

As you move forward along your path of love, of living and expressing love, more and more of this personal power is available to you as you ascend, as you master your lessons, living according to the highest possible potentials of your life, the highest possibilities for you here and now, directly connected to the Divine.

Retaining your awareness of this connection with all of life, with the source, and with All That Is, return awareness to your physical being, to this present time where you are focused, alert and more energized than before, ready to take action, to live inspired, to walk your path of love one step at a time.

I am Archangel Michael and I am always pleased to connect with you, to assist you and guide you. Link first with Source and with All That Is and then invite me in. I am ready, willing and happy to assist.

You are so loved, blessed and encouraged upon your path.

# 14

# Activation of
# Spiritual Awareness
## ~ *Archangel Uriel*

*G*reetings. I, Archangel Uriel am now present. I offer healing and a vibrational pattern of thought centered in Divine love and spirit, and compassion for all beings, with a purpose to elevate your mind and to infuse your energy and awareness with Divine love, presence and awareness. Experience the fullness of sensation and meaning through this connection – a link which now bridges the spiritual and physical planes and unites all into one for the purpose of illuminating your heart and mind, uniting heart and mind and spirit for your well-being, by transcending the experience of struggle which is tied through *attachment* to what is or what has been.

Release what no longer serves you – but not in terms of letting it go so that it is no longer present, for energy cannot be destroyed. Release what no longer serves you by releasing your attachment  to it. Release the power it has to impact you in a negative way, and release your attachment to outcomes, to desires, to challenges. Release your judgments on what has been, on past actions and choices, prior failures and struggles. Release your attachment to future possibilities, probabilities and potentials. You are claiming the power in energy and frequency and spirit to be fully aware, to perceive and be present in this moment.

Release your attachment to what has been or what will be. These cords are cut and the truth revealed – that now is all you have been and all you will be. It is within the present moment that you will find your power, your heightened abilities of awareness, your heightened ability to perceive beyond the physical dimension in a way that is neither abnormal or supernatural, in a way that is essential for bridging nonphysical and physical realms, to anchor the higher dimensions into present time – but not for our benefit. We are present in these higher dimensional energies of love and light always, but your realm, your plane, your Earth has been bombarded for eons with lower vibrational frequencies transmitted purposefully for control, leveraging the darkness for the gain of a few. Now you are able to inspire all to leverage the power of the light and of positive thought and spiritual vibration.

To infuse these fine vibrations of light and love into your essence changes your point of magnetism. Your thought sphere, emotions and beliefs combine and influence what you create and experience in your life. And so as you allow yourself to be uplifted in the Divine white light, in the Divine love of the spiritual realms, you contribute to the collective unconscious, and consciousness, infusing the energy of blessings into what is being created from within this point of Now.

The present moment now is where your full vibrational power returns and your spiritual awareness and perception beyond the physical opens so you can witness what encompasses past, present and future. All directions of time are present now as one field of energy, all interconnected, and mirroring your inner state of being through your outside experience.

Peace, joy, love and harmony are broadcast your way now. Think yes to allow these Divine frequencies to infuse your being, awaken your senses and inspire your potential.

You claim through willingness, persistence and focus the ability which has always been within your grasp, to impart blessings upon all. You are able to manifest blessings in your life and then allowing blessings to overflow outward towards others, releasing humanity from the shackles and confines of guilt, jealousy, superiority.

Tune into love and recognize your oneness with all beings. Offer your forgiveness to those who have harmed, judged or angered you in anyway. Receive forgiveness on behalf of all those, including you, who you have harmed or caused hardship for in any way.

Through forgiveness you make space within your Self to be infused and awakened with light to positively transform this Now, this point of power, now where you are able to love, to serve, to shine, to live vibrantly and passionately in peace, acceptance and awareness.

With these qualities of the Divine infused in your energetic signature, your choices and actions will be more naturally in alignment with the service of all life. This alignment will move humanity and Earth into a positive era of awakening, collaboration and co-creation. Rewrite the potential future by infusing your present moment with love which will serve greatly to prevent hardship, collapse and meltdown for many.

Consciously choose a new possibility. Release your attachment to the fear energy which spirals throughout consciousness. Choose to embrace the vision of love which begins with your life, and the lives of all those who you are able to reach and benefit. This love then ripples out through all of consciousness and brings about healing at an intrinsic level. Your love inspires blessings and know that these are yours to create.

Breathe freely now as many ascended masters and spiritual beings – your team of guides and angels – assist you in releasing your attachment to that which does not really matter and which no longer serves. When you let go of who you were and even who you are now... You make room for who you might become.

Think or say... "With assistance from the Divine and from the angels, I Am now canceling, clearing, and releasing all that no longer serves me into the light. I release all that I have been, and all that I think, perceive and believe about myself and who I am. I cancel, clear and release into the light all which is false, limiting, and untrue so I may more fully step into who I might become in love and in authentic truth"

Attune yourself to the Divine love, magnificence, well-being and gratitude that is present here and now, that is the direct route for fully awakening your senses. Love which increases your awareness, opens your eyes, activates your light and inspires your being.

Respond with love and infuse the present moment with love to serve Earth and to serve all life. Through love in the present moment you are able to make a difference now. And with this intention to love and serve, your spiritual power that was drained from you during past lifetimes is now able to finally return. Personal power, spiritual power, and all aspects of Self across the lines of time return to you now cleansed, awakened, and purified for the highest and greatest good so that you may serve with Divine love and compassion, with willingness, with integrity, with honesty and with intention.

Know that you are supported, you are loved and you are uplifted. Enjoy this elevated frequency and know that it is only the beginning. You are now able to achieve new heights as new activations occur at the cellular and genetic level from working with the Divine, from working with your guides, with your angels, and with love and light.

Your DNA is activated, your senses awakened, your heart inspired, your mind clarified, your passion realized, your truth authenticated, your heart on fire: awakened, present and centered in Divine love.

Breathe freely and anchor this energy of Divine light activation, frequency and blessing into your Now, into your body, mind and spirit. Accept your power and expanded sense of awareness. Breathe, relax, receive and know you are able to make a difference through love and service. All the power of the light and of Divine frequency is accessible to you. Knowledge, wisdom, truth and well-being are accessible within every moment.

I, Archangel Uriel, deem this to be true. I leave you now with a final infusion of light. Accept, breathe and awaken. The fire of the Divine light burns brightly within you. Shine, love and live fully. For now I am complete. And so it is.

# 15

# Align with Divine Guidance

## ~ *Archangel Michael*

*I*ndeed, I am Archangel Michael and I greet you with divine downloads of compassion, radiant joy, well-being, and peace. Relax your mind and body. Relax the senses by which you normally perceive the physical realm. Focus upon your breathing and upon these words. Receive these downloads of divine frequency to uplift your vibration and to attune your mind, body and spirit to perceive and sense.

Psychically view, hear, sense and know the love, guidance and wisdom present in these words and beneath the surface, spoken to your heart, transmitted energetically to soothe and to bring about rejuvenation of your being to purify and enlighten your spiritual self, and to assist you in embracing the gifts of the Divine which are bestowed upon you.

Your unique combination of spiritual gifts and abilities allows you to accomplish your Divine soul mission and purpose, your Divine blueprint and path. Do not worry if you cannot see your entire path before you, for you're walking it and it appears one step at a time, one choice at a time, one moment at a time. Being able to move forward into the unknown without knowing precisely where you are going or what you will encounter is the lesson of being human, of learning your way through life, of growing, evolving, and boldly and confidently moving forward. Take action, take your next step, commit, choose and progress forward even without clear certainty, but doing the best you can.

Follow the nudges of your heart, the guidance of your soul, and take action. Your soul smiles upon this regardless of the outcome. Your personality sees your life's lessons and moments through the lens of duality: good or bad, hope or fear. Your soul sees the middle path as being in between these polar opposites, being rooted in learning, evolving and moving forward. This is a huge part of your purpose – simply learning and growing your way through life for within each choice and opportunity lies the potential for growth and lessons. Yes, there are more specific aspects and tangents of unique and Divine gifts and purpose. You are present here to learn and to share these. By boldly and confidently choosing to move in the direction that brings you personal joy and fulfillment through positive service and helping others, you naturally and Divinely align with the specifics of the purpose of why you are here.

There are also things you can do to increase your clarity of knowledge, to increase your certainty, to remove the haze and align with clarity. Nature holds magnificent healing powers of alignment, of healing, to align you with information, with guidance from the Divine and from your soul. And so time in nature serves you immensely in knowing your purpose, for in your time surrounded by the natural world, embraced by the love of all life, guidance can clearly shine through. Remove yourself often from the buzz of your world, economy, television, internet, screens, cars and life. Be at peace and perceive the intricate dance of the

Divine present in the natural world.

Meditation serves you greatly inside and out. Whether you are in the city or in the forest or out in the countryside, wherever you are you can remove the distractions and the buzz for a time by surrounding yourself with Divine white light, deeming it so, entering in, going deeper, and relaxing further. Consciously breathe and choose to experience silence, stillness and calm. This takes practice. Indeed, but know that it is a stepping stone on the path to awakening your fullest gifts, whatever they may be. You are unique as are your gifts. And so while there is much information about the psychic senses being contained within five spheres of influence: sight, thought, knowing, hearing and smelling, each of these is expanded much further.

The point in this is that your way of perceiving beyond the veil, your way of perceiving in the realm of spirit is uniquely yours. You may be trying to see clairvoyantly in a certain way when your guidance is effortlessly flowing in through your feeling, knowing, imagination or through visual cues from the physical world, or through certain sounds or ideas or triggers.

The lesson is to quiet your mind and become aware. Keep a journal of your spiritual experiences that you can look back on. This will help you to distinguish what is true guidance from your soul, from your angels, from your guides, from your loved ones, and what is thought, mind, or even telepathic interference from others present in this physical world.

You can receive information from the collective consciousness, from another physical human being, or you can receive direct guidance from spirit, from God, or from the angels. Awareness, practice and persistence will help you to distinguish where, how, and in what way information from the Divine flows through you.

You are a translator of the vast field of consciousness. You absorb an infinite amount of information and focus it in a way you can understand. For most of your life you've been focused on translating this infinite realm of possibility through your physical senses. Open further your psychic and spiritual gifts, practice tuning out physical senses and focus on breathing, on the space within, on quietude. And out of this inner stillness and calm, knowledge, guidance and sensation will appear.

Your resonance plays a role in the amount of spiritual information you are able to receive as well. If you're focused on worrying, if you're focused on doubt, if you're focused on guilt, you are a million miles away from the unconditional love and compassion that your angels are broadcasting. And bridging this gap will require effort.

Surround yourself with joy, love, peace, and compassion. As you take control of your thoughts, your sphere of influence, and your personal energy signature you are able to infuse your personal vibration with Divine love, light and frequency through intention and awareness. If you like I will assist you in infusing your personal vibration now with Divine white light. Simply think, and repeat silently or in your mind, "Divine white light now fills my aura. Divine white light now fills my energetic signature, I radiate Divine white light."

Imagine now an orb of light above your head that shines down upon you, uniting first the *chakra* energy centers of your physical body in a column of white light, balancing, healing and activating these energetic centers, and removing blockages at the physical or spiritual level therein. Your *chakras* assist you in translating the infinite oneness of the Divine through your unique gifts and lens of perception. And so as light from the Divine shines down, feel it gather in your root *chakra* area, your base which grounds you, and activates your sense of wholeness and well-being. Your root *chakra* is the base for your other energetic centers to build upon, it is the foundation which fuels the fire of your spiritual gifts and abilities. Your base, your root *chakra* is healed, purified and balanced now.

Imagine Divine white light continuing to pour down upon you, washing away residue, releasing tension, struggle and doubt, aligning you with the Divine love and gifts that are your authentic truth and birthright. This light now gathers in your sacral *chakra*, your center of Divine joy, your fluidity in relationships, your sacral *chakra* is now balanced, purified and activated. Soul blockages, toxins and tension are released. This center is purified with Divine clarity and love. Often called the seat of your soul your sacral *chakra* is the home of your intuition, and is activated and awakened now with Divine white light that continues to flow down from above, uniting all your *chakras* as one.

Now focus upon your navel, your solar plexus *chakra* and the home of your personal power. When balanced this *chakra* allows for ease in your emotions, knowing your true identity and aligning with your inner Divine wisdom. The white light within and all around you now purifies toxic emotion and limiting beliefs, releasing all that no longer serves within this *chakra* energetic center into the light. Realigning you now with Divine power, balance and emotional ease and well-being.

The Divine light continues to flow all around you as you read these words, releasing doubt and fear, releasing toxins and blockages, and now focusing upon your heart, healing away guilt, self-blame, self-hatred, and grief. Activating, balancing and purifying the message center of your heart which enables you to directly perceive guidance from the Divine, which enables love to flow in your life, which enables the flow of love from the Divine into your experience.

Open up, and allow your heart to be purified by a heart healing – a cleansing of past wounds, of feeling unloved. These feelings melt away and you are overcome with the feeling of being loved by the Divine. You are love and you are loved, and your heart center is balanced and purified now.

Divine light focuses now upon your throat *chakra*, your communication center and your action center. Allow the light to unify this, to strengthen your ability to listen and to communicate, to speak Divine truth, clearing out harsh words and perspectives, aligning Divine communication with Divinely inspired action.

Light flows down all around you and focuses now upon your brow *chakra*, your third eye. The light brings healing to your mind, releases clutter and haziness, releases the unbalanced running of the mind, activating this center, activating clarity of mind and offering an ability to sense and perceive beyond the physical and to peer into the realms of Divine love.

Light flows all around you washing out residue, toxins, density, and increasing your vibration, building out your aura, and now focusing upon your crown *chakra* at the top of your head, activating this center, purifying your connection with the universal source, your connection with the Divine. Your crown chakra is your filter for Divine information, when balanced allowing clarity of Divine guidance to flow in. Light flows here now purifying this gateway, allowing universal consciousness to enter into your experience, your spiritual body, emotional being, mental body, and physical being.

Your crown chakra is purified and opened to allow a new level of Divine light to flow in, which now unites all these *chakras* of your physical body in a column of white light, which extends upward now.

Go up in consciousness, float up, way up, into the light, the light above, into the presence with Divine source, and with All That Is.

Relax, breathe, and feel the blessings of the Divine imparted upon you. Feel the healing light which unites with your energetic and physical being. Feel the gifts of the Divine being bestowed upon you. Feel your clarity for perceiving in the Divine realms increased and attuned.

Relax and know that as you relax in the presence of the Divine, healing, rejuvenation and well-being are automatically absorbed and conveyed. Embrace this healing, embrace this Divine love, embrace this well-being. Open up to your gifts and to your light. Be willing to stand in your truth, in your power of the Divine, in your authentic truth – as the magnificent spiritual being that you are. Be willing to confidently move forward, to move out of hope into action, out of fear into knowing that whatever you choose, you are learning, you are moving forward, you are progressing and this is your gift in being a physical being, in learning the lessons of life, in evolving forward, progressing forward, loving your way forward.

Divine joy, love, compassion, rejuvenation and well-being are infused into your spiritual, mental, emotional and physical being.

And now as you return awareness to your physical body, retain the perception of the realms of the Divine. Retain the infusion of Divine light in your aura. Support turning onto a new page, support yourself in a beautiful new beginning by consciously choosing to remain in love, by staying positive, and knowing that it will work out, that you are supported, that you are guided, that you are loved.

As you practice elevating your vibration and linking with the Divine, your clarity improves and your gifts increase. Your clarity of purpose becomes more known. Keep taking steps, keep moving forward, continue taking action with gratitude for what has been, for the many goals and objectives you've already accomplished, for those who have served and loved and assisted you in your life. Give gratitude and this gratitude further amplifies your personal power and your Divine ability. Gratitude increases your frequency.

And so with love and gratitude in your aura, with light, with joy, and with love, choose to celebrate your life as it is now – a learning, evolving, ever-unfolding process of experiencing the full power of the Divine and of your spirit here in the physical realm.

You have so much support available to you. Increase your light to tune into this Divine love. I am Archangel Michael and I leave you with a final infusion of Divine light, of gratitude, of well-being, of rejuvenation, and of love. Embrace these blessings and now act and take your next step forward. You are so loved and blessed and uplifted. Shine and make a difference, for you hold this power. For now I am complete. You are so loved.

# 16

# Spark of Divine Light

## ~ *Archangel Michael*

Greetings, dear one! Indeed, I am Archangel Michael and I greet you here and now with Divine love, with light, and with uplifting frequency which you can begin to tune into by simply relaxing, quieting your mind, and focusing within. Focus inside now on your inner being and tune into the light of the Divine.

You are able to access the nurturing, rejuvenating and healing vibrations present here and now which you become blocked from when you are in another state of mind, another way of thinking – but your remedy is simple. You have the opportunity here to reset your emotional atmosphere, and to infuse your entire being with Divine love.

Know that all is well, that you are safe, that you are surrounded with benevolent beings in spiritual form – angels and guides of the light, ascended masters of unconditional, divine love and presence – and you are surrounded with pure, white light of the Divine and All That Is so when you focus within, simply focusing on your breathing and letting go, relaxing, and entering in, you are able to naturally integrate the light and the presence of the Divine, the unconditional love here and now which infuses your entire being with the blessings that love brings.

And so imagine you're breathing in white light now, first into your lower abdomen. Breathe in the white light and as you exhale, let go and lift higher. Now, breathe into your upper abdomen, breathe in the white light, and as you exhale let go and lift higher. Now breathe into your upper chest and as you exhale, let go and shine brighter. And now simply breathe naturally, relax, and with each breath in fill yourself with Divine light, and on your exhale lift higher, shine brighter, tune into more and more of the Divine light, and increase your radiance.

Continue to breathe as you recognize in this moment that you are ever connected to the Divine and with awareness of the Divine light which is all around, aware of this connection through your inner being, through your heart and through your soul. As the infinite blessings of Divine love become available to you, and the increased radiance you carry with you becomes know, you cannot help but overflow love and blessings to those you care about and to those you don't even know.

Your increased vibration positively impacts all. This is again made possible through simply focusing within, relaxing and breathing in the light of the Divine. Become aware, and be open to lifting into a new level of light. Infuse your entire being with Divine love, align yourself with the elevated frequency that is broadcast your way, and is present here and now. Breathe, relax and lift.

At this time, notice an orb of Divine light above your head which pours down in a column of light, activating the energetic center at the top of your head. This is your spiritual center, your crown *chakra*, your direct link to the Divine that is cleansed, purified and activated now. Divine light, white light is pouring all around you, elevating your being, paving the pathway between you in this here and now, in this present moment, and the infinite love and blessing of the Divine that is possible for you to achieve in this life through stepping into fully embodying, being and living as Divine love manifested through your experience.

And so link with this Divine presence through your crown *chakra*, through the spiritual center at the top of your head. Be bathed in the Divine white light which flows in and all around, elevating you now, effortlessly lifting your vibration, attuning you to Divine love, cleansing and clearing, and preparing you to step back into living with increased radiance, to living more closely aligned with your higher self, manifesting Divine love through your words, actions, presence, and through your being.

This light continues to flow into your being. Let go and enjoy this experience of Divine light, for ultimately you are one with the light of the Divine and one with all. And by tuning into that here and now, by becoming aware of that oneness here and now, your oneness with the Divine becomes easier to recognize. In addition, each being you encounter is also one with the Divine, and therefore one with you.

And so treating others as the Divine beings they are regardless of race or religion or status or regardless of their current actions and beliefs and limitations. You are through your oneness with the Divine able to see that spark of Divine light present in the darkness illuminating everything with the power of the light. This awareness of the Divine energy present here and now and always paves the path for you to rise higher and for all – for the collective, for humanity as mass consciousness to become increasingly aware of this oneness and love and interconnectedness.

And so while lasting, positive change in your world may seem far off at times, remember that through your connection with the Divine you are able to positively impact and influence all. Start by simply linking with Divine love and manifesting as this brilliance and presence of positive change, progression and increased awareness, and the inner light others cannot help but to be revealed. For through this connection to the Divine and to All That Is, you are one and so your growth, awareness and love has a lasting impact and offers a powerful way for you to create change on a grand scale to benefit all. In what may seem overly simple by being, breathing, going within, linking with the Divine, breathing in light, lifting higher, and radiating light outwards, you are serving all beings.

And if you want to take this a step further, hold a vision of an awakened humanity, of an enlightened Earth, of collaboration and co-creation. Hold this vision for those who have no hope, for those who cannot see, for those who get pulled into the dramas of ego, which you yourself may experience from time to time, and which is fine, just return to love.

Reset your energetic signature. Infuse your vibration with light, with frequency, with presence, with knowledge, oneness, and with the direct experience of the Divine so that this is what you contribute, this is what you energetically manifest: Divine love. Let this be what you emanate outward and draw unto you: Divine love.

Manifest Divine love through your presence, your awareness, and through radiantly shining your light. And so as you once again become aware of the Divine light that is all around you, which illuminates you, which uplifts you, which makes you feel good, which empowers you, which strengthens your aura, which cleanses your energy, which activates your potential and opens your spiritual gifts and abilities, know that this light is always present. This Divine presence is always present in every moment, in every object, in every person, at every time.

Your task, your opportunity is to become aware and to tune in, to look deeply, to hold focus, to be present, to see the Divine in nature, in your brothers and sisters, in all of humanity, in animals, in everything. The more you are aware of the Divine light flowing throughout all, the more you integrate it into your being, and the more you positively contribute vibrationally through love and through frequency, which creates change. A small ripple in the field of infinite possibility expands outward indefinitely in each moment through your return to love.

Breathe in the white light and as you exhale, shine. Breathe in the light and as you exhale, lift higher. Breathe in the light and now as you exhale, return your focus to your physical being –glowing, radiant, and present. Notice that you can retain this awareness of the Divine even as your rational, logical mind shifts back on again. You can retain this presence and awareness of the Divine as you wash dishes, as you do your work, as you drive your car, through all of your life.

Return to love, return to awareness, return to presence, return to noticing, to honoring, to experiencing, to being the spiritual being that you are, that is one with the Divine, with I, Archangel Michael, with your team of guides and angels, with all. We stream a final blessing of love and gratitude your way, and invite you to receive this blessing of Divine love and light and gratitude.

Receive this energetic blessing and let it emanate outward now and pass it on, to create a small ripple energetically at first, which will later compound, expand and manifest itself in a real and tangible way. For energetically aligning with the Divine holds the potential to truly empower positive change and transformation for the highest and greatest good.

# 17

# Divine Alignment

## ~ *Archangel Haniel*

Greetings, beloved one. Know that you are, indeed, in the presence of many guides and angels of the light at this time. I, Archangel Haniel, speak and we angels blend our energy together now and surround you with the insight, wisdom and healing power of the Divine.

The energy of the Divine is perfectly balanced in masculine and feminine light. It surrounds you and uplifts you in vibration. Imagine this light of the Divine all around you now. Imagine it above your head and below your feet. Imagine breathing in the light and as you exhale, let go of thought, let go of worry, let go of your grip upon the physical world. Let go and enter in.

Breathe in the light and as you exhale, focus within. Imagine an orb of balanced masculine, feminine Divine light appearing above your head and beginning to shower down upon you. Divine light cleansing your vibration of all that has been, cleansing your beliefs and thoughts and patterns about who you are, and releasing all that no longer serves into the light. This cleansing white light, flows down all around you and assists you in grounding your energy to the Earth Mother in this present moment, grounding your energy down through the floor. A crystal column of white light flows down all the way to the core of the Earth where you connect with a beautiful light therein, a healing energy of the Divine Mother, nurturing and rejuvenating your being.

Feel the unconditional love present at the core of the Earth and experience your oneness therein. Breathe deeply and relax. Notice and be aware of your oneness with the Earth, with the light at the core of the Earth and with All That Is. And now imagine this light is streaming upward, up and in through the bottom of your feet, up through your legs, through your calves and thighs and hips, activating and clearing your root *chakra*, your sacral *chakra*, your solar plexus *chakra*, continuing up along your spinal column through your heart *chakra*, your throat *chakra*, your third eye, your crown *chakra*. A crystal column of light flows up through your entire physical being and cleanses and activates, initiates and illuminates you from the inside out as this light flows upward.

Go up with it now. Lift up, way up into the light, lift up into direct presence with Source and with All That Is. Go up, lift up, and notice the Divine light present here, the energy of God, of Divine masculinity and femininity, of light, of unconditional love which is all around you, the energy of Source. Experience the oneness present throughout All That Is which illuminates you now, which uplifts you higher, which inspires blessings and positive changes in your life.

Imagine this light now surrounding your physical body. Feel, sense, be aware of this light around your physical form and imagine that it is now expanding to encompass your emotional, logical, spiritual body and expanding out further to fill the room you're in. This Divine white light is all around you and continues to expand, to fill your entire home, to fill your entire neighborhood with the light of the Divine.

Divine light cleansing out all that no longer serves, cleansing out the old and the blocked and the stagnant, cleansing out all that is not truth and all that is not in alignment with Divine will and love. Imagine this light continuing to expand outward around your entire town or city, around your entire state, around the entire country you are present in now. Divine light blessing all who are held within it. And now imagine the Divine light surrounding the entire planet Earth, cleansing, uplifting and blessing all who are within, all who are a part of this unique energy, this one planet, this one Earth.

Receive a Divine cleansing and blessing now and imagine that this Divine light is expanding to contain your entire solar system, galaxy, universe. Divine light surrounds you and now expands outward so far, wide, tall and deep that it embodies and surrounds All That Is, and all that you are a part of. You are tuning into the entirety of your being, of your greater self, of your Divine self who is one with Divine masculine and feminine, who is one with All That Is. And through this awareness, connected to the Divine and connected to the energy of unconditional love, you are able to bless all now by simply focusing upon your heart, allowing the light to fill and illuminate your heart, and now imagining that the light in your heart, the sacred flame of the Divine present within you bursts open to expand outward around you flowing throughout All That Is.

Breathe and be aware of this flow. Be aware and let go of all that no longer serves, by simply thinking "Yes," as we now affirm on your behalf. "I now release, clear, cancel and delete all patterns of thought which do not ultimately serve. I now clear, cancel and release all aspects of myself which are not ultimately true and which no longer serve."

Release all limitations, release density, release all that no longer serves according to Divine will into the light for the highest and greatest good. And so it is. This Divine cleansing of your being occurs across the lines of time, across the many multiple dimensions you coexist within, across the multiple realms of space, throughout all of existence.

You are cleansed, purified and uplifted now so that you may begin anew, so that you may begin fresh, re-energized, re-inspired to live authentically and true to the Divine spiritual being that you are. What does this look like? You may wonder – *how does this manifest?* Indeed, through being aware of the Divine light which flows throughout everything, which flows throughout all of creation, and that you are a part of, you are able to notice the blessings and the beauty and the inspired Divine design. You are able to in a moment return to living in alignment with the original blueprint of Divine love, releasing the limiting beliefs and constructs of separation, of competition, of superiority, and recognizing that Divine light is present in everything, in every moment, at all times.

And when focused upon, this Divine light is able to rise to the surface, to manifest, and to be created in beautiful, inspiring, joyful ways to heal, uplift and renew that which has been weighed down through density. There is a great opportunity now to become illuminated and completely transformed. You have the opportunity now to become completely transformed, to change in the most positive way, to flow with the universe in the direction of positive change not fearing what is unknown, but walking the path of love forward to meet your destiny, to accomplish your purpose, your soul mission, and to bring your spiritual gifts to the surface – the gifts inspired within you by the Divine so that you can make a difference through your every interaction and action in the present moment.

Your gifts needn't be elaborate or even known or understood by others. And by simply following your passion, following your bliss, serving with love, your gifts will naturally open, blossom and unfold. You will naturally contribute according to Divine will for the highest and greatest good. And this contribution will bring you fulfillment and joy and abundance and love, for this is the original blueprint for creation within the physical realm. And this is what you as humanity are moving towards, moving out of the paradigm of separation, greed, duality and fear, moving into the realm of synchronicity and into the flow of abundance and love.

In this present moment, wherein masculine and feminine are united in the Divine, are united in the present time and together in their Divine dance are able to create in the manner which will most serve all of life and all realms. Your choices as an individual ripple throughout all of creation and have an impact across the globe and across the cosmos. For Earth reuniting with love not only benefits the Earth but benefits all beings and all realms across all dimensions and all lines of time. This is one of the many reasons why there is so much support available to you on Earth now – support available for you to claim your unique gifts and your unique opportunities, for this is the realm where you have the opportunity to live in multiple dimensions simultaneously, in the realms of mind, body, spirit and emotions where you have the opportunity to live and create in the physical, mental, astral, spiritual, and digital planes.

Here you have the ability to create with your mind, with your physical actions, with your spiritual intentions empowered through your positive emotions around what you want to create. Ultimately it is on the path of love that you infuse Divine blessings throughout all of existence, creating the greatest contribution at this time.

You are able to create significant and lasting change in your life, which benefits the lives of others, which heals your reality, which transforms the present, which paves the foundation for a positive, rewarding, fulfilling and inspiring future that you are able to move in the direction of, into living vibrantly well and fulfilled. You are able to move into the direction of vibrantly thriving by simply taking your next step.

From within the present moment, notice the blessings of light which are present in all. Claim the blessings of the Divine present in the light of the moon brightly shining down upon you, with the energy of renewal and of Divine love. Present in the energy of rain washing down around you, carrying the Divine energy of love and cleansing, and in the gentle wind carrying the energy of Divine light cleansing your being, and present in the Earth below your feet carrying the Divine light and offering you a foundation, and in the energy of fire carrying the Divine light, transmuting your worries, fears, guilt and grief into the light. The energy of wood carries Divine light, the trees hold the space of Divine presence, creating fresh air for you to breathe, and the energy of metal carries Divine light offering the opportunity for you to build and create in the physical realm.

All of creation, all of Earth, all that exists carries Divine light within. And it is this dance of the Divine, this expression of the Divine in its many forms that you are here to play within, to enjoy and to experience. And, indeed beloved one, you are here with a unique mission to assist a world out of balance in returning to Divine love, a world out of balance in returning to a state of balanced masculine and feminine. Divine balance is grounded in Divine love. This moment is your opportunity; the time is now.

As always, you are the one with the ability to create change. Take your next step with love and with a willingness to err, with a willingness to not get it quite right. Just take your next step and the next will follow.

Continue moving in the direction of your goal, in the direction of your becoming, in the direction of living fulfilled, inspired and in alignment with the full light of the Divine manifest as your higher self, one with the Divine and one with All That Is and connected to you as a physical being in this present moment. Step into living as the full embodiment of the Divine present in physical form. This is your ascension path and through this, you are able to positively impact all for the highest and greatest good according to Divine will. And so it is.

# 18

# Experience the Flow of Love

## ~ *Archangel Metatron*

$G$ reetings, beloved one. Indeed, I am Archangel Metatron and I greet you in this present moment with Divine healing, love and frequency. You are surrounded with Divine light, and you are in the presence of your guides and angels. You are blessed, uplifted and supported in turning inward now. Focus within. Become aware and tune into your energetic being, the underlying flow of Divine energy which flows throughout your being, which rejuvenates your body, uplifts your mind and empowers your spirit.

This flow of energy along your spinal column expands outward now to fill in your aura. When the flow of Divine energy is unblocked and allowed to flow freely, it is able to expand further to fill your light body with unconditional love and light of the Divine. This uplifts you further and serves as a vehicle allowing you to travel into higher dimensional realms and planes of existence to link with higher consciousness and to establish this enlightened perspective, Christ consciousness, Divine consciousness within the physical realm in the service and love of all of life, of all souls, and of All That Is.

At this time, tune into your energetic flow. Notice below your feet an orb of white light or golden light representing the light of Earth which is, of course, one with the Divine light of all. This light flows up through the bottom of your feet and up along your spinal column passing through seven energetic centers, the *chakras* of your physical body. Each energetic center governs attributes and qualities of your life. When blockages are present within one *chakra* the Divine light is unable to continue to flow, unable to bring rejuvenation and healing and higher vibrational energy further into your physical, mental, emotional and spiritual being, your light body.

And so while you may desire to open your upper energetic centers and we often speak of opening your heart, this cannot truly be accomplished without letting the light flow through your lower *chakra* centers first – your base.

At this time, imagine Divine light flowing up through your being. Light flowing up and in through the bottom of your feet, up through your first three main energetic centers, red, orange and yellow. You are assisted by your angels and by I, Metatron, in letting go of blocks, tensions and frustrations held within any of these energetic centers. Let your blockages release into the light, allowing the light of the Divine to flow up so that this light may fuel the flame of your heart. At this time open your heart and release any blockages held therein.

Allow the Divine light to continue up to your throat chakra, up into to blue, indigo, the violet of your third eye and up into your crown chakra, and the white light above your head. The Divine light flowing up connects you to the Universe above, to the Divine, and to All That Is and then pours back down, flowing down along your spinal column, filling out your aura, your energetic being, your light body.

Light flows up from the Divine light at the core of the Earth, to connect you with All That Is. Let it rise up along your spinal column and overflow above you, and then light pours down to fill out your energy body, elevating your frequency, and rejuvenating your being. A strong energetic being and balanced flow of energy keeps you healthy, centered and connected to the Divine. This flow of energy and your connection to the Divine is strengthened through unconditional love.

Unconditional love, the energy of your heart chakra which vibrates with the beautiful color green, is only possible with the lower *chakras* overseeing additional facets of love like security, relationships and contracts are balanced. With your lower chakra energy centers open and unblocked, unconditional love is able to sweep through your life. The energy of love protects you and uplifts you further, aligning you with the inspiration available for you.

Love makes possible the direct link with the Divine and with your guides, with your higher Self, with your soul. With love in and around you others are not able to block your energetic flow. The external world cannot block your ever-present link with the Divine. But you can in your reaction to what is external, block the flow of light, and this is a common way to become blocked up.

Energetic blockages lead to manifestations such as illness, fatigue or low energy mentally, emotionally and spiritually. An energetic blockage can also lead to frustrations, anger and impatience, judgment, guilt and grief. These are the emotional states of being which block your energy centers and block the flow of Divine light and love through your being. Fear blocks the flow.

It is important to love in every moment, to respond with love, for the energy of love enables light to continue to flow throughout your being. And in maintaining this sort of flow energetically you naturally rise higher into an enlightened state of consciousness. Awareness is required to choose love in the moment and awareness is a a precursor that serves you. Become aware of the awareness you are tuning into in the higher realms.

When you are in love and when you allow Divine frequency to flow freely throughout your body and energetic being, you are in harmony and resonate with with loving people, loving situations and interactions. You may be greeted by an entity or being who chooses not to walk in love, who chooses to walk in fear and density and negativity, and in this sort of greeting is often called a psychic attack, when the energy of negativity bombards your energetic atmosphere. But as we mentioned, no one can block your energetic flow other than you. And so when greeted by an entity centered in negativity, fear or density, it is simply your reaction that causes the block and the stoppage of the flow of Divine love. And yet if you feel this anxiety coming on, if you feel scared or tense or worried as a result of the energy of another coming into your energetic space, and you respond with love, love acts as the most powerful sort of protective shield you could possibly have.

In the case of negative entities, they'll simply move on to a being who they are in resonance with, for love is not in resonance with fear. Hatred and negativity and darkness are gently but oh so effectively repelled from your energetic state of being with a simple shift in perspective and a return to love in the moment. In this way, love and joy become the most powerful psychic shield you can wear for it naturally protects you against beings who are not in resonance, who may not have your highest and best interests in mind. And it ensures that in your interactions, you are only delivering the most uplifting, positive, loving, rewarding and rejuvenating energy to others. And so karmically you are in alignment with positivity and with love and with remaining helpful to others, true to your mission as a soul here on Earth and able to move forward in life towards your next lesson. So an encounter with a negative entity is a sort of test. Are you able to respond with love and be unaffected? This is always the case when your response is love. Or are you yourself pulled into the drama of density, fear and darkness, which then blocks the Divine flow through your being, prohibiting the Divine light from traveling up through your lower chakras into your heart where you are able to receive and express and live unconditional love.

When the powerful energetic center, your heart, is left unfueled by light of the Divine this can manifest through blockage and cause the experience of pain or sorrow. But love flowing freely through you, in and around, and through your energetic being protects you. It uplifts and inspires all whom you encounter, and it keeps you in alignment with your path and purpose.

At this time I, Metatron, form a metatronic cube around you. It is a Divine star, a *merkaba* of light and of healing, of purifying energy. This light energy forms around you and begins with an overall clearing and uplifting of your aura and your light body.

As this Divine sacred geometric form spins slowly around you, it is like a towel being rung out. Any blocks or negativity or energy which are not yours in your aura and light body will be released into the light of the Divine.

And now the sacred geometric form shrinks in size and moves down below your feet. It begins to move up your spinal column while continuing its spin, moving up slowly and gently, cleansing the energetic pathway along your spine of any negativity or blockage.

Your root chakra is cleansed, balanced and purified, allowing light to flow through. Your sacral chakra is cleansed, balanced and purified, allowing the flow of light. Your solar plexus chakra is cleansed, balanced and purified, allowing light to continue to travel upward. Your heart chakra is cleansed, balanced and purified by this divine *merkaba* gently spinning and lifting upward. Your throat chakra is cleansed, balanced and purified and the *merkaba* of Divine light continues upward. Your third eye chakra is cleansed, balanced and purified. And your crown chakra is cleansed, balanced and purified. This merkaba star now leaves through the top of your crown chakra, continuing up into the light.

Imagine your energy overflowing now after the light of the Divine has traveled all the way up through your energetic form and now overflows in a waterfall of Divine love around your being. As this happens, the light continues to flow upward along your spinal column and then pours down around you filling out your aura and your light body.

Your angels work to ever so slightly adjust your auric field with unconditional love, strengthening the barrier of your aura so that you are able to retain this Divine light flowing up through you and pouring down all around you, strengthening your auric field, revitalizing your energetic being, uplifting you, empowering you, rejuvenating you, healing you, vibrationally attuning you to the Divine love present here and now. Illness and injury, anxiety and negativity, tension and challenges result as your energetic being does not resonate with the sometimes harsh physical vibrations present in this world. Your response to this harsh energy may cause a blockage in you. Uplift yourself now and uplift that which was dense. When you love, negativity is released, is filtered out, and is effortlessly dissolved.

At this time, your energy is functioning beautifully. The light flows up and pours down. This cycle has a Taurus-like effect flowing up, down, filling in around you, overflowing beyond you so that you are able to serve others by simply sharing your love and joy. For when love and joy are shared each benefits the other and returns to you cleansed and purified, further strengthening your energetic form, further elevating your vibration and increasing the levels of consciousness you are able to tune into.

Imagine your aura and your light body now completely filled with the light of the Divine. When this is the case, you are able to travel in consciousness into the higher realms, lifting up in consciousness to link with your higher self, with your guides, with your angels and directly with the Divine to tune into the perspective of unconditional love in every moment, to tune into the higher cosmic teachings available to you at this time in this life, in this sacred journey you are walking. It is a journey to serve and to love, to maintain your energy, to assist others and to grow.

Your opportunity here is huge and vast. Yes, at some point you will leave your physical body and return to the spiritual realm and at this point you will likely remember and think, "Wow, I wish I would have done more. I wish I would have taken advantage of my opportunity in life to serve, to love, to evolve as a soul and become a conscious co-creator with the Divine in service of all life. We say this to you so that you make the choice now to make the most of this life, to maintain your energy and to assist others in returning to love.

How do you do this? Through love.

Allow the light of the Divine to flow through you and consciously choose to react in the present moment, to serve others, to respond to life, to fill your being, to infuse your consciousness with the love of the Divine, which is present in every moment and when tuned into blossoms through the expression of your life. Unconditional love manifests through a smile, through patience, through compassion, through consideration, through understanding, through listening, through service. Unconditional love soothes and rejuvenates your being. Unconditional love heals and inspires. Unconditional love allows freedom to flow through your being and to overflow to others, aligns your next steps, keeps you on track, aligns you with your purpose and with your opportunity here and now to love, to make a difference, to serve, and to evolve as a physical being, as a spiritual being, as a soul. Simply through choosing, allowing and experiencing the flow of love.

Yes, you must witness pain and negativity in others at times, but when you do and when you respond with love, that density is transformed. In a small way at first, into a subtle or unconscious way at first, but with practice, with persistence and with consistency, love manifests miracles. Jesus is known to have completed many miracles. Not he as a physical being, but he as a soul simply allowing unconditional love to flow through – that is what empowered all these miracles to occur. Loving everything can miraculously transform and realign everything, bringing Earth and humanity into vibrational resonance with unconditional love and with the Divine.

And through this, much of the current traumas and tensions and challenges and illnesses and struggles you collectively experience will be resolved and healed through you choosing love and through this love inspiring another to choose love, to respond with love, to allow love to flow through. The ripple effect unfolds, the tipping point is reached, and the mass return to love is possible. This is the new age, this is the new Earth. This is the new energy that is anchoring here and now.

Consciously, personally, and collectively walk the path of love, live and love, allow the Divine love and light to flow through you. Consciously choose to continue releasing blockages as they occur and responding to density as it occurs with love so that all are positively transformed.

I, Archangel Metatron, encourage you to be aware and to notice how you feel now that you have been infused with the love of the Divine. Do you feel uplifted, and empowered? You are.

Return to this empowered perspective in every moment. Consciously choose to be a beacon of love, a lighthouse of truth, a ray of bliss, serving through love, empowering others through love, living your authentic truth on your path of love for the highest and greatest good for your benefit and for the well-being of all.

Let love grow and build, blossom and bloom. Let love flow, for you are love and are connected to infinite love. And when unblocked, when love is let free, all things are possible. Indeed, I leave you now with love and with my blessing.

# 19

# Integrated Healing

## ~ *Archangel Michael*

Greetings, beloved! Indeed, we are here – I, Archangel Michael, speak, though many are present to offer healing and frequency now. This healing will begin in the mental realm and plane. It occurs by infusing your thought forms and consciousness with Divine love, with thought patterns of vibrant well-being and health empowered by a clear, focused and balanced mind.

Understand that when your mind runs and races, this make it possible for you to absorb negativity from others, from the collective mind, even if your thoughts are mostly positive. Take control of the mind through awareness, through self-presence, and through focusing and ensuring that the energy you are attracting is in alignment with the Divine healing, well-being and vibrant living that you consciously desire.

Many say they desire health and will focus on manifesting health, yet continue to experience challenges. As you master meditation, the skill of mind focusing and control becomes your tool every step of the way. One ancient form of magic involves working with the realm of thought to infuse your thought patterns and your personal atmosphere with positivity for your own benefit and for the benefit of all. This service of all souls is a form of working with what has been known in the past as "white magic." And any darkness of magic simply comes from negative thoughts or wishing negative things upon others.

Ultimately, for your well-being, indeed, the white magic and positivity which benefits all will infuse your entire being with frequency and blessings from the Divine. Indeed, as you serve, love and forgive others, as you express and radiate gratitude, awareness and presence, then health and vitality will naturally flow into your being.

It is true that when you relax and link with the Divine, healing and rejuvenation come into alignment and are merged with your being. And so Divine frequency is broadcast to your mental being now: Divine downloads of clarity, love, peace and serenity for a clear, collected mind. These are present here and now and provide an important foundation for the integrated healing of your physical, mental and spiritual bodies.

These healing downloads now attune your mind to your heart and to the Divine mind and offer you the ability to see the blessings, oneness and love present at all times.

In a similar manner and fashion, we offer now emotional and spiritual healing to assist you in dissolving blockages at the soul and cellular level to increase your light energetically, and prepare your physical body to receive rejuvenation, healing and light as you simply relax.

Breathe freely and let go of tension, self criticism, grief and guilt. Embrace these blessings of healing and light we flow your way to receive them. Breathe and receive the Divine blessings broadcast now from the angelic realm – they are downloaded and bestowed upon you, and integrated into your being with love, presence and awareness. This healing can expand and align you with more vibrant living in every aspect and meaning.

We invite you now to plant a seed of thought: *I am vibrantly healthy. I am well. Well-being is my natural state. When I relax, my physical body is rejuvenated and healed by the Divine.*

Relax, breathe, and know that this healing is real. Simply reading these words and allowing for the possibility brings healing light for your personal, physical, mental, emotional and spiritual well-being. It is powerful and it is Divine.

As you relax and read, a healing energy flows throughout your body and dissolves blockages and tension, preparing your entire being for your onward journey, for your next steps forward, for your path forward into awakening, into love, moving forward on your path of learning and uniting with spirit, with the Divine, with everything.

Before we leave you now, we send a final surge of vibration, of healing and Divine essence. Receive this vital well-being, this presence, this awareness and Divine love.

# 20

# Oneness

## ~ *Archangel Metatron*

*B*eloved one, indeed, I am Archangel Metatron. I greet you now in a vortex of Divine light and love, in a vortex surrounding us both and lifting you up into a place outside of time and space, into the ever-present Now to tune into the infinite supply of light, frequency and Divine healing to fill your body, mind and spirit with the unconditional love broadcast from above.

Breathe freely and relax. Feel your vibration lifting, feel yourself expanding now. Allow your consciousness to reach out into the room around you. Recognize that you are one with your surroundings and one with all. Think upon your city and the state where you reside and recognize your oneness with everything contained within. Your oneness on this larger sort of scale can be understood by recognizing that, indeed, it is your greater self who is infinitely one with the Divine light, your greater self who is infinitely one with God, with the energy of All That Is flowing throughout everything.

And so when you are ascending, when you are lifting up into new levels of vibration and light, you are essentially aligning with your greater self, your higher self, the self which is connected to

All That Is and you are thereby able to recognize your oneness with all.

Think upon the earth as one, as one cell making up the Earth, making up all who inhabit the Earth, all who live upon the Earth, all the plants and animals and minerals, the very atoms and fibers of creation, of the natural world – all this is your greater self.

Feel your oneness with the Earth and with All That Is. Feel your oneness with your greater self. Think upon the cosmos, the constellations and stars shining down on you from above. The stars each have their own solar systems revolving around and which are contained within galaxies of vast magnitude. Recognize your oneness with all, your oneness with the heavens above, with the cosmos above, with the Earth, with All That Is.

From this expanded perspective, from this awakened perspective through recognizing your oneness with all, you are able to positively impact all. As you choose love in the present moment you create a ripple of love, of positive energy through the greater consciousness of All That Is.

This ripple effect happens automatically by default, but with awareness of yourself and this vast scale you are creating within, you may be more committed to positively influencing and impacting all rather than simply thinking in a small sense that you are separate and that your actions influence your life alone. This couldn't be further from the truth.

You are vast, you are expansive, you are one with everything and through your actions and intentions your energy impacts All That Is. This is true in the sense that your inner world, your inner realm and state of being influences what you see in the greater universe around you. And this is true in the sense that you are able to positively impact the world around you through shifting your inner world. This is true in the sense that all of creation – the entire universe – is ready and waiting to conspire with you to accomplish your goals and dreams.

When you allow for this possibility in your belief system and your conscious state of being in this here and now, outside of time and space, anything is possible.

By being aware of your greater self and through this aware of your connection with this greater consciousness and one-ness within everything, you receive a blessing of Divine love, a blessing of Divine frequency, a blessing of illumination which emanates outward from your present place, which emanates outward from where you are now, and flows throughout all. For you, a being of light, connected to all that is receiving a bless-ing of Divine love, automatically deliver this beyond you. You receive love and through this automatically send the blessing of Divine love to all.

You may focus this, yes, and receive the blessing of Divine love in through your crown *chakra* at the top of your head, which flows down your spinal column through your physical body and flows back out from your heart, from your portal of sacred love, flowing out through your heart and your hands to the Earth, to humanity, to the plant and mineral and animal kingdoms, to the stars and spiritual realms, to the cosmos and galaxies, to parallel and alternate dimensions, to all aspects of yourself, all multidi-mensional aspects of yourself that exist in alternate timelines, parallel experiences – realities which have played out in parallel dimensions where you chose in other ways, where you began to initiate something and stopped in this life, but it continued on in that parallel reality.

As you receive Divine love now recognize that you are one with all, with all of this we speak of, with All That Is, with the angels, with I, Metatron, with your higher self, with higher consciousness, indeed, with Christ, the Divine feminine, Divine masculine, with everything. Your awareness of your oneness with this and your awareness and willingness to act with this unity in mind, to treat your neighbor as yourself, to see your greater self present in all, to notice people in your experience as expressions of the same oneness is infinitely powerful.

You are my other God self. I am your other God self. We are one with each other; we are one with all. Let this perspective influence your actions, allowing a willingness to serve the greater one emerge, rather than a limited perspective of only wanting to help yourself and your inner circle. Ultimately, your circle encompasses all.

And so take care of the Earth that you are part of. Take care of the ocean that you are. Love the neighbors of yours that you are. Love the humanity that you are. You are one with each, you are one with all. Open your heart to love yourself, to love all, and to realign with the infinite possibility of your life made possible through awareness and oneness with your greater self, which carries a complete Divine frequency, a frequency which is completely Divine.

You are loved, blessed and uplifted. Radiate this love, share this love, shine this love upon all whom you meet, for you are one. You can even take this a step further to silently bless those who you find yourself judging, to bless those who you align with on your path, not verbally or publicly, unless you would like, but simply by thinking:

*I see the divine in you. I see the divine in me. I allow divine blessings to flow into both of our lives through my open heart, for we are one.*

This (A) reminds you to open your heart; (B) reminds you to link with the infinite supply of Divine love; and (C) aligns the other at their personality/self level with the Divine love and with the energy of oneness.

I am Metatron and you are my other God self. We are one. I leave you with my blessing, with a blessing of oneness, an awareness of the Divine God/Goddess flowing through all, flowing throughout you, and one with All That Is. See the miracle present in this day, the beauty in this moment, the Divine flowing throughout All That Is.

# 21

# Unlimited Love

## ~ *Archangel Uriel*

G reetings! Indeed, I, Archangel Uriel, greet you here and
now. I draw your awareness to the increased amount of
light and Divine energy all around you. I will assist you in aligning
your vibration so that you may receive these crystalline light codes
of the Divine, so that you may integrate the increased light into
your being.

*Why?* You may wonder. Light aligned with your body, mind and
spirit now increases your vibration and serves to align you with
the greater vision of what is possible for you to accomplish, for
you to contribute, for you to experience within your lifetime.

For whatever you have done, for whatever you perceive yourself
to be, however far you have progressed, however high you have
risen, there is a further point, there is forward progress available
to you still. There is upward illumination, there is deeper progress into the energy of enlightenment, ascension, increased vibration, personal evolution, and alignment with your higher self
and spirit, with your greater self and spirit, with Divine spirit and
pure light, pure bliss, pure unconditional and Divine love which
is able to be anchored into your being in this lifetime.

And so tuning into the magnificent energies of this light

now present is made possible through your open heart and through your willingness to turn away from mind, to turn away from thought, to turn away from mental chatter, worry, stress, guilt, grief, blame and tension.

Let go of the density you have experienced in the past. Let go of the thoughts which spiral around you in the present. Enter into the space between these words. Enter into the space within you. Open your heart, quiet your mind, breathe, and energetically feel yourself drop in. Feel your awareness turning inward. As if you're traveling downward, traveling down a staircase into your inner being, traveling into your inner world, your inner realm, traveling in, opening your heart, and entering in.

It is from this inwardly focused perspective that you are then able to lift consciously in light on wings of angels and ascend the staircase of light, lifting in vibration into the realms of the Divine, into the realms of angels, into the realms of light, into direct presence with Source, with God, with All That Is.

Let yourself now lift in vibration, in energy, in light. Your team of guides, guardian angels, saints and ascended masters surround you now. We adjust and attune your energy so that you may unite directly with the Divine light, so that you may lift and experience the bliss and wonder, the wisdom and healing and light of the Divine realms now, so that you may merge consciously and unconsciously, spiritually and energetically, mentally and physically unite with the oneness and love, with the Divine light that is present all around. Divine light which when focused upon can build and increase in strength and light, and beautifully unite with you here and now.

Breathe deeply and feel the beauty, the uplifted energy, the oneness you are a part of, the oneness with the Divine which you are able to experience, feel, sense, see, know and witness now. Notice Divine white light all around you. Breathe in the light. Exhale and let go. Breathe in the light. Exhale and step into the flow of Divine love, of Divine oneness, of synchronicity which is able to manifest unlimited blessings in your life and your path.

Breathe in the light which aligns your body, mind and spirit with your highest and greatest good. Breathe in the light, exhale and let go of your limitations, your tensions and your fears. Breathe in the light. Breathe in the Divine energy of love. Breathe in the well-being, the energy of thriving, the love, and let it cycle through your entire being as it uplifts your mind, body and spirit, cleansing your slate, cleansing the remnants of what has been, cleansing the painful and challenging emotions tied to the past. Let this energy cleanse out the feelings of satisfaction and accomplishment you have experienced as well as the feelings of frustration and failure. Whatever you have or have not been, whatever has been and has yet to manifest is cleared.

A new beginning, a blank slate, an opportunity is presented to you now to begin again, to reflect on what you have and have not accomplished in your life, and to raise the bar, to elevate into the light, to rise into a grander vision and dream of what is possible for you in this life, of what is possible for you to experience, contribute, serve, create and manifest, for you are unlimited when you fully align with the Divine spirit that you are. Fully aligning with your full Divinity and light is your life purpose, this is your greater purpose on a broad scale.

And through this union with the Divine, through this place of elevated vibration and oneness with everything, the intricate aspects of your purpose can be detected. You can know and experience and see that you are able to create lasting change, that you are able to serve and love in a way which awakens you, excites you, fuels your fire, and which benefits all. This Divine alignment is possible.

Let yourself now receive a vision, an idea, an inspiration of the greatness which you can experience in this life. Yet understand that aligning with the full light of your spirit is purpose and service in and of itself, but then through this Divine union, through the full manifestation of love in your life, your every interaction becomes empowering to yourself and others. Your every action serves, uplifts and assists.

When you express the love that you are, when you recognize the love that you are, when you live in love, as love, mindful of love, then the blessings of love elevate the entire playing field. Love elevates the current paradigm, elevates the vibration you radiate and elevates the vibration which is mirrored back to you.

And so you see the energy is present, the love is here and now it is simply the ego mind and the tight grip upon past beliefs, upon past ways of living and being which block you from the full experience of Divine love, of the new paradigm, of the new Earth, of light, well-being and vibrant bliss. Your embracing this now in this moment, and moving forward returning to love in the present moment, returning to love when you experience lower vibrations, when you get pulled into drama and tension and frustration will allow you to confidently stand in the light.

Release what no longer serves you and return to love. This changes everything, changes the game you play, changes the life you experience, changes the magnitude and scope of the service you are able to contribute, of the difference you are able to make, of the life you are able to live and the lives you are able to touch.

Love and light, bliss and joy and radiant well-being are all around. The elevated vibration is present here and now. The higher realms have opened their doors, the higher dimensions have lowered their veils.

And as you peel back the layers of filters blocking you from this love and light, as you peel back the layers and filters blocking you from diving into the higher realms, you are able to merge with the Divine. This begins through your conscious and unconscious meditation and moves in to fully experiencing higher realms present within the realm of Earth at all times, in all places, in every moment.

This is your grand purpose, your general purpose for being here and now, your labor of light as a spiritual being in physical form, as an ascending being on planet Earth, as a Divine spirit creating within the physical realm.

From the perspective of a limited being, the truth is you are unlimited. As you align more and more with love in the present moment, you open more and more to the light and love which is all around you. You remove barriers, you open doors, you pave the pathway for others, you ascend, you serve, you inspire, you align with the Divine love that you are one with, and you become able to recognize this oneness within you and within all which changes everything. This changes your point of perspective and your point of creation, which changes how you respond and relate to the world, which changes how the world responds and relates to you.

The new paradigm of love has begun, it is here. Let yourself enter in, step into your role as a way finder, as a leader, as an ascending initiate, as a being able to experience the blessings of this new frontier which are accessible in every moment, accessible by releasing the filters and layers of doubt, releasing the blockages and tensions within.

When you notice a mental picture, an emotion, a vibration, a belief, a blockage, an energy which you are carrying which is not love, feel it and release it into the light. Hand it over to your angels where it is dissolved into Divine love. Then breathe in love and light, elevate your energy, shine and glow, be one with the flow of Divine light, of Divine well-being, of radiant, authentic, magnificent love and bliss.

I am Archangel Uriel and as I leave you, I send a final surge of love in your direction to cleanse and elevate your being. This opens your energetic receptors so that you become aware and can perceive and notice and align with the blessings of Divine love, light and synchronicity which are always around you, and which when tuned into, acknowledged and focused upon manifest further, increasing in frequency and intensity.

Love is the new paradigm you're stepping into, one moment at a time. You are loved, supported and assisted – your team of guides and guardian angels surround you now with their love, respect and encouragement, and provide whatever energy you most need that will most serve you now in letting go of what has been, and in dreaming a new empowering dream for your future. Know that with love it is possible to accomplish the desires of your heart and soul, to serve, to make a difference and to live as the full expression of Divine love and spirit in physical form.

Dream consciously of the blessings you can create with love and take steps one at a time to contribute and to bring yourself and others into alignment with the love that is all around. Love is within you and when tuned into can accelerate and open up to you even more. This Divine love, light, bliss and well-being are yours. Focus within, rise upward and experience this now.

The present moment provides all the power you need. It contains an infinite supply of Divine love and light. Let go of your ego mind, enter into your heart, take your next step, and know that you are so loved, supported, assisted and uplifted by the entire universe – by the realms of spirit, by your team of guides and angels, by I, Archangel Uriel, and by the very energy of light, of the Divine and of love, by All That Is.

# 22

# Maintaining An Increased Vibration

## ~ *Archangel Metatron*

ᏱᎧᏆᎧ᠍ᏫᎧᏱ

G reetings, dear one. I am Archangel Metatron and I greet you now. You are greeted and surrounded with Divine love and frequency with a team of your guides and angels who assist you now in rising up in vibration to embody more of the Divine light, the personal creative power, the well-being and vibrant energy that you are able to access at any time, that becomes your authentic essence as a spiritual being.

And so take a deep breath and enter in. Let the light at the core of the Earth flow up. Up through your *chakras*, up into your open heart, up into your throat, your third eye and crown. Up into the light where you connect with Source, with All That Is, with the Divine, in this place where your spirit is cleansed and uplifted, your body balanced and rejuvenated, your mind calmed and focused.

The Divine healing frequency is all around you and when you invite it into your experience, knowing that it is available in an unlimited supply, you naturally cleanse your being and uplift your vibration. Understand that uplifting your vibration is, indeed, part of your greater ascension. Uplifting your vibration allows you to access your spiritual gifts of intuition, of psychic ability, and allows you to access your guides and angels in the higher realms. This increases your creativity, productivity, your physical vitality, and your energy, your joy, your ability to love, to be well, to live vibrantly, and to thrive as a human being.

Uplifting your vibration need not be something abstract. Understand that your ever-unfolding ascension, this raising of vibration begins to impact you automatically and has a positive effect. It does not neutralize every challenge remaining before you, nor does it make your life incredibly easy so you can float through on autopilot. You will continue to be challenged, but understand that it is often through challenge that you experience the most growth and the greatest opportunity to raise your vibration further.

You are here as a soul in this present moment to take a quantum leap in spiritual growth, in awareness, in ever-unfolding understanding. You are a spiritual being, your ascension process is becoming aligned with this truth. Clearing your vibration, your mind, body and spirit, lifting up to experience the Divine realms, setting your intentions, staying focused, taking action, following your intuition, and living the path of joy and love are of paramount importance.

But I speak to you now about maintaining an uplifted vibration for, yes, it is true that you are able to reach new heights and if you are not aware, come crashing down to lower lows, which ultimately does not benefit you as an ascending being.

You want to be able to make steps incrementally and maintain your vibration at each step along the way. You are able to do this, you are able to maintain it by keeping a sense of balance. Balance your work in the physical realm with meditative time in the spiritual one, balancing work and play, balancing action and inaction, doing and being, speaking and listening – balance in all areas of your life is key to maintaining an increased vibration.

There are, of course, situations and people and circumstances which will cause you to lose your balance. This is, quite simply, a part of your life experience. And our advice to you is to dance, to bend, to sway, to be flexible, to go with the flow of life which you have stepped into, to allow, and to respond in the moment according to love and in line with your heart's desire.

There are also measures that you can take to energetically protect yourself from many outside negative influences, to protect your expanded vibration, your increased frequency in order to maintain these new levels of love and light, which benefit not only your own life in so many ways but also create a positive ripple throughout All That Is.

It is worthwhile to elevate your vibration, and increase your light, to build your aura and your light body, to expand consciously and to maintain this expanded perspective. It is worthwhile to maintain your higher vibration and frequency.

Divine light, white light, is useful in many ways. It is useful in cleansing your being, uplifting your vibration, and, indeed, protecting your mind, body and spirit. And the difference in using the light of the Divine in these different ways is simply using your intention:

*Divine white light, surround me now. Divine white light, cleanse me now. Divine white light, uplift me now. Divine white light, help me to balance now. Soothe me now. Comfort me now. Heal me now. Protect me now.*

Visualize an orb of white light around you. This is one of the most widely taught and known methods of protection, and for a good reason: it works. This Divine white orb shield does not allow negativity to pass through. It protects your aura and vibration and keeps you from absorbing the negative energy of others, or density in any form, or any malicious or malintended thoughts or entities or vibrations which are headed your way. When they encounter the white orb, this shield of light, they are automatically dissolved and released into the light of the Divine.

You are protected, you maintain an uplifted vibration, and rather than acting as a wall and allowing nothing to pass through, the white orb shields your mind, body and spirit and yet allows love, compassion and guidance to flow through from your team of guides and angels and ascended masters. So the uplifting, joyful, vibrant energies of love are able to align with your being so that you are able to continue to grow and evolve and expand in consciousness and in frequency while avoiding negative entities and energy. By wearing the shield of light you actually release negativity of all forms into the light. It is a form of protection and light work in one.

In the morning, when you wake up, when your energy expands as it naturally does whenever you transition from sleeping to wakefulness, imagine a white light orb around you. This is a wonderful meditation to begin your day, for it automatically increases your light. Wearing the light orb raises your vibration, for light of the Divine is filled with the qualities of the Divine which are positive and represent love, joy and harmony. Wearing these vibrations like a cloak with the light orb around you, the shield of light around you, makes these qualities accessible by you.

And when you go to work, or into a store, when you are walking close to someone who is stuck in a line of negative thinking and action and perhaps your guard is down, you can get caught up in thought, caught up in a negative thought which normally would draw the negative thought of the other towards you and invite it into your experience. But wearing the light orb, putting it on in the morning and intending that it stay with you throughout your day, gives you protection. You are able to maintain your positive vibration in the midst of negativity – in the midst of chaos, confusion, crowds, and density.

Protection is essential for maintaining your vibration. Calling upon Archangel Michael for protection is always welcome and I, Archangel Metatron, am happy to assist with protecting, indeed.

If you ask, I am pleased to place my Metatron's cube around you in addition to the orb of white light for an extra layer of uplifting, inspiring and protecting frequency.

Let's practice with this now.

Think or say, *I call upon a white light orb of the Divine to surround me for protection. Remain with me throughout the day, and I call upon Metatron's cube with the assistance of Archangel Metatron to surround the light orb for an extra layer, which repels negativity and density in all forms into the light and which allows love, well-being, guidance, healing and light to pass through. I intend this for the highest and greatest good to maintain my vibration and to uplift my energy further. And so it is. And so it shall be.*

This simple invocation can be modified and changed. Make it your own, and use it on a daily basis in one form or another to protect your vibration.

Now, are there shortcuts? Yes.

But practice building the elaborate protection shield in this way. Visualize it around you, imagine it protecting you, and then if you are in a pinch, if you forget to put it on and suddenly find yourself in a crowded, chaotic, negative situation, you can simply think or say, *Protection now.*

Imagine this multi-part shield around you and so it shall be. If you practice calling it in, and visualize it around you, and meditate upon it every day, it will be there when you need it, time and time again.

You have completed much cleansing already, but a part of maintaining your vibration is continuing to cleanse yourself on a regular basis. Even if you wear the protection shield all day, your own internal compass, thoughts and fears may attract some negativity and density and there may be old things which come up for you, which vibrate at a lower rate than the high vibrational being you're stepping into.

Here is another meditative practice, and we say meditative practice but with a clarification. This can be done in 30 seconds or in three minutes, quickly while you brush your teeth, while you take a shower, or when you lie down to go to sleep at night. Imagine a waterfall of Divine white light flowing around you, cleansing your being.

*Divine white light, cleanse my being.*

I offer you one additional vibrational tool for your tool belt to maintain an increased vibration and to continue further on your ascension path. This is best done sitting or lying down. Become still, focus within, open your heart, run your energy – that means allow the light at the core of the earth to flow upward, clearing and balancing all your *chakras* on the way up, uniting all your *chakras* in a column of white light, and rise up in consciousness to link with the Divine:

*I now invite the full vibration of my higher self and spirit to download into my being – mind, body and spirit – for the highest and greatest good.*

If you are seated or lying, imagine now the magnificent light of your higher self merging with your being. Imagine that your mind, body and spirit are a glowing, vibrant, incredibly high-vibration being – a Divine soul, a Divine spirit which is downloading into your being now, merging with you now, cleansing, uplifting, balancing you for the highest and the greatest good, aligning you with the higher vibrational qualities of your soul, with the power of your higher self, with the healing and well-being, rejuvenation and uplifting energy available to you now and at every moment. Notice if there is a color or quality of the Divine which appears in your consciousness, a quality of the Divine which your higher self is focused upon manifesting.

What is this quality? Tune into it.

Notice how you can embrace this quality more in your life and it will help you to live more authentically, truer to who you are as a soul and as a spiritual being. Feel your energy lightened, uplifted, vibrating at an increased rate through this merging with your higher self.

Allow the energy to flow up through your being and allow the light of the Divine to flow down through your crown, through your third eye, throat, heart, solar plexus, sacral region and root, to cleanse, balance, purify and align all these energy centers with Divine love, and to flush out anything which is negativity or which does not serve.

Feel your energy grounding downward now, light flowing down through your legs and feet through the layers of Earth below you, flowing down in a column of white light to the core of the Earth.

Experience your oneness with the Divine light of Earth and All That Is, and now complete the loop by letting the light of the Earth flow up through the layers of Earth, through your feet and legs, up the column of light along your spine, the column of white light uniting all your *chakras* as one.

Open your heart and let its flame brightly shine. You are a magnificent spiritual being in physical form, and you have all that you need to ascend, to vibrantly live, to love, and to make a difference one moment at a time, one step at a time.

Know that you are loved and supported and that the team of guides and angels around you embrace you now, bringing you whatever it is you most need – energy, a message, healing, guidance to help you continue on in this journey of life, moving in the direction of mastery, of love, and of living as your authentic, spiritual being, high vibrational, vibrant, thriving, and so it is.

As I Metatron, step back, your guides and angels, your inner circle and team take a step forward. They will meet with you, uniting with your soul, with your higher self and spirit, aligning that which is needed to manifest your highest and greatest good, encouraging you to take the action steps with are required to bring about your dreams and goals, soothing, rejuvenating and loving you fully and completely. And so it is.

Let your awareness return to your physical body and to the increased vibration and energy you are now carrying. Know that you can maintain this light in a balanced, grounded and centered way that benefits you and serves all. You are guided, loved, supported and assisted. I leave you with my blessing.

# Bonus .MP3 Meditation

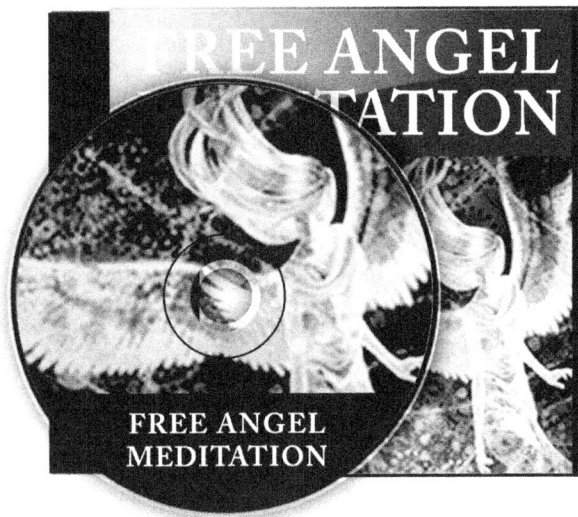

*D*id you enjoy reading these Ascension Angel Messages? If so you may really enjoy the experience of listening to the .MP3 audio recordings.

Get a free angel meditation channeled by Melanie here:
http://www.Ask-Angels.com/light

# About the Author

**MELANIE BECKLER** is an internationally acclaimed author, spiritual teacher and clear channel of the light.

Through walking the path of an open heart, Melanie has remembered her direct link with the Divine and angelic realms. She feels both honored and blessed to share the ever-unfolding and expanding guidance, love and uplifting energy that flows through as a result of her direct connection with the realm of angels.

Melanie remains focused on publishing the empowering teachings from spirit to assist humanity and earth in the ascension process.

# Connect with Melanie
## at her website

www.Ask-Angels.com

Or Connect with Melanie on Social Media:

facebook.com/askangelsfan

youtube.com/askangels

twitter.com/askangels

instagram.com/melaniebeckler

# Also by Melanie Beckler

## Let Your Light Shine

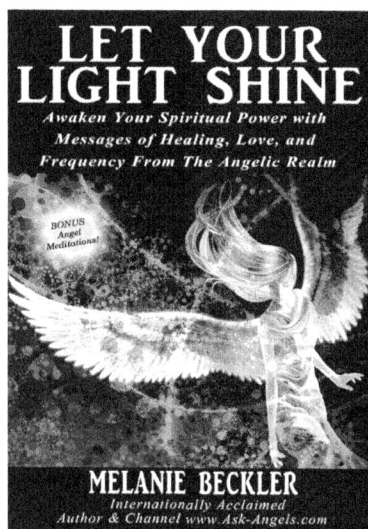

*Open your heart and mind to experience the unconditional love and guidance of the Angelic Realm. Simply reading these messages from the angels will assist you in bringing more joy, healing, and spiritual fulfillment into your life. With the guidance and uplifting angelic frequency woven throughout these pages, you will be inspired, to Let Your Light Shine!*

http://www.amazon.com/dp/B00AA59U9W

# Experience Angels

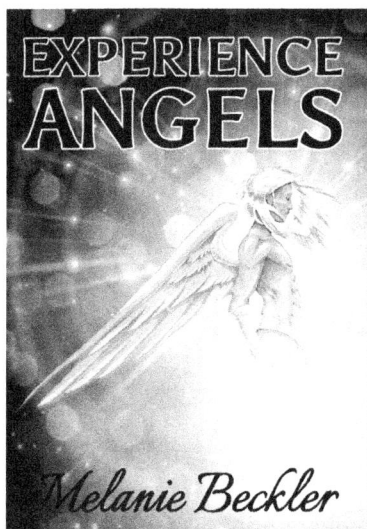

Experiencing angels is simple once you know how to make the connection. Simply relax and read as Archangel Uriel, Archangel Metatron, Archangel Michael and the Angelic Guide Orion walk you through the process of activating and opening your chakras, lifting your vibration, and connecting with your Guardian Angels. Then rise even higher to experience your Higher Self and the realm of the Archangels. This book will help you pave the pathway so that you can directly connect with the Angelic Realms, to Experience Angels for yourself.

http://www.amazon.com/dp/B00G8UVIAM/

# Angel Messages

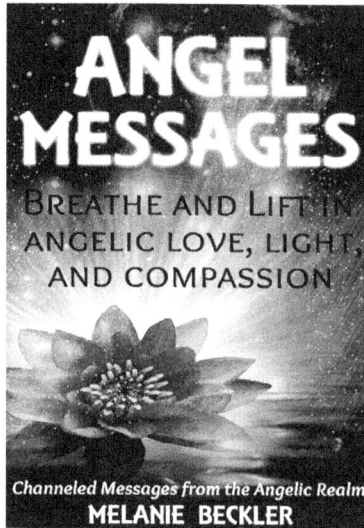

*Manifesting blessings in your life and the lives of others is an important aspect of your true purpose here on Earth. As you build up your spiritual light, you are able to more easily share positive blessings and you become more protected from the negativity of every-day life. By reading these angel messages and tuning into the angelic frequencies they contain, you are able to connect with healing and bring more joy, love and abundance in to your life.*

http://www.amazon.com/dp/B00BB8XLCE/

# Ask Angels Oracle Card App

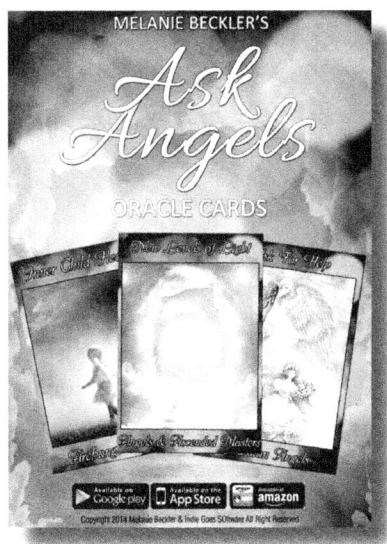

*The angel messages found within the Ask Angels Oracle App will help you to lift in love to connect with the guidance, healing, and wisdom of the angels. The Ask Angels Oracle cards are based on the angel messages channeled by Melanie Beckler, and carry with them the uplifting frequency and presence of the Angelic Realms. Whether you are seeking to elevate your mood or ask your angels for help and guidance, this oracle app can deliver just that.*

http://www.ask-angels.com/go/askangelsoracle/

Printed in Great Britain
by Amazon